Building Enterprise Applications with Windows® Presentation Foundation and the Model View ViewModel Pattern

Raffaele Garofalo

Published with the authorization of Microsoft Corporation by:
O'Reilly Media, Inc.
1005 Gravenstein Highway North
Sebastopol, California 95472

Printed and bound in the United States of America.

1 2 3 4 5 6 7 8 9 LSI 6 5 4 3 2 1

Microsoft Press titles may be purchased for educational, business or sales promotional use. Online editions are also available for most titles (http://my.safaribooksonline.com). For more information, contact our corporate/institutional sales department: (800) 998-9938 or corporate@oreilly.com. Visit our website at microsoftpress.oreilly.com. Send comments to mspinput@microsoft.com.

Acquisitions and Development Editor: Russell Jones
Production Editor: Kristen Borg
Production Services: Octal Publishing, Inc.
Technical Reviewer: David Hill
Indexing: Fred Brown
Cover: Karen Montgomery
Illustrator: Robert Romano

978-0-735-65092-3

To my wife Deborah. Thank you for everything!

Contents at a Glance

Table of Contents

What do you think of this book? We want to hear from you!

Microsoft is interested in hearing your feedback so we can continually improve our books and learning resources for you. To participate in a brief online survey, please visit:

www.microsoft.com/learning/booksurvey/

Introduction

The Windows Presentation Framework (WPF), Silverlight, and Windows Phone 7 are the latest technologies for building flexible user interfaces (UI) for applications built with Microsoft technology. All three rely on the XAML markup language to describe UI elements and layout, and you can program applications for all three platforms with the most common of Microsoft .NET Framework languages: Visual C# or Visual Basic .NET. If you are a .NET developer planning to create a new Line of Business (LOB) application using the .NET Framework, you should consider adopting one of these technologies as your UI technology. At the same time, as you start planning to build an application based on one of these technologies, you should also seriously consider learning and applying the Model View ViewModel (MVVM) presentation pattern, a design pattern created specifically for these technologies.

And that's what this book is about. You might be wondering, "Why another book on WPF?" Or, if you have already looked at the Table of Contents, you might be thinking, "Why another book about layering and design patterns?"

To answer those questions, let me start by saying that over the years, I have noticed that what developers ask for the most is not the "Bible of patterns" or the "Bible of how to layer an application;" instead, they want a simple, straightforward book that guides them through the development criteria for a real-world, yet simple, application that *uses* and *explains* patterns—but that is also reusable in future projects as a "template" for other applications.

WPF and Silverlight are young technologies, and the percentage of developers moving to this new way of designing the UI is still small. There are several reasons for this. First, the learning curve is relatively high. If you're used to Windows Forms, Java Swing, or Delphi, the way you design and structure an application using XAML and WPF is significantly different—in fact, I would call it "revolutionary."

In the past, I have used well-known patterns to build applications, including the Model View Presenter pattern with Windows Forms applications, and the Model View Controller pattern with ASP.NET applications. But with WPF, these two approaches are now obsolete, because they can't take advantage of the powerful engine provided by XAML. Of course, you can still take advantage of the binding engine of WPF using the Model View Presenter pattern, but the effort required is usually too large. Fortunately, MVVM provides an alternative.

Microsoft, in collaboration with some architects, has revised the original Presentation Model that was proposed years ago by Martin Fowler. This revision (named the Model View ViewModel pattern) is the perfect approach for WPF and Silverlight because, well, it was designed specifically for them! Unfortunately, like XAML, MVVM is a relatively new technology, so at the moment, there isn't a lot of information about implementing it. There are a few bloggers trying the MVVM approach and blogging about it; others are involved in building MVVM-specific toolkits. But nearly everything is still experimental, and there are few truly concrete examples.

Therein lies the rationale for a book about building a LOB application using MVVM. As you proceed through this book, you will see examples that show how to build a straightforward Customer Relationship Management (CRM) program with WPF 4, Silverlight 4, and the MVVM pattern. The book guides you through the entire architectural process, illustrating the correct approach to using MVVM. You'll also use some other new technologies delivered with Microsoft .NET 4, such as Managed Extensions, Windows Workflow Foundation 4, and of course, the Entity Framework.

First, you are introduced to the tools. Next, you move ahead to build the CRM, starting with the domain model, applying a simple technique to persist the data in a relational database by using two of the most popular Object-Relational Mapper (O/RM) systems available for .NET: the Entity Framework and NHibernate. Then, see how to make everything more flexible using the MEF framework.

Following that, you learn to apply business logic and data validation to this model in a way that fulfills the requirements of the MVVM pattern. In this phase, you also look at Windows Workflow Foundation (WF) 4.0, the powerful, new workflow engine by Microsoft, and study the steps required to build a simple workflow engine.

The remaining chapters all focus on MVVM. There are four major concepts that you must learn to use MVVM correctly: *commanding*, the *template*, the *binding engine*, and how to *orchestrate* everything together. At the end of this process, you will have visited all the layers required to complete a classic LOB application, but more importantly, you will be able to recycle the parts described here as a template for building future applications. Of course, there are some differences between WPF and Silverlight, so this book will try to cover those gaps where possible.

Finally, you will take a brief tour of the MVVM toolkits that are already available, such as PRISM, a composite application framework for WPF and Silverlight. This will help you to determine when and how you should use each as part of the process of building a small and flexible MVVM framework.

Overall, the key goal of this book is to provide a complete step-by-step guide for using WPF/Silverlight in conjunction with MVVM for creating generic code that you will be able to use and reuse in the future.

Building Enterprise Applications with Windows Presentation Foundation and the Model View View-Model Pattern provides not only a solid analysis of how the MVVM pattern works and how to apply it with WPF and Silverlight, but it also offers an exhaustive guide to building layered applications by using the most common and accepted techniques. This book intentionally doesn't show *all* the related code for any given project; instead, it focuses more on the principles and patterns that developers should apply to create well-structured and easy-to-maintain LOB applications.

The book analyzes each layer that composes a LOB application, starting with the Domain Model (also known as the Business Layer), moving to the Data Layer (including an overview of Entity Framework and NHibernate), and ending with a chapter dedicated to Business Rules and Windows Workflow Foundation. Of course, you will also find a chapter dedicated to the MVVM pattern.

In addition to the patterns and practices explained in the book, Chapter 7 contains a useful list of open source frameworks and plug-ins used by others in the .NET community to build applications that implement the MVVM pattern with WPF or Silverlight.

Who Should Read this Book

This book is for any .NET developer or software architect who wants to learn how to build LOB applications using well-known enterprise architecture patterns, including the MVVM pattern. Readers should already have a solid general knowledge of programming, be familiar with the overall purpose and application of patterns, and of course, know WPF, Silverlight, or Windows Phone 7. While the book touches all these topics, it doesn't attempt to teach basic programming or pattern application principles. Instead, it's aimed at developers and architects who have already built .NET applications and are now moving toward designing and building enterprise applications with .NET.

Specifically, this book targets WPF or Silverlight developers who already have experience with one or both of these technologies, but who don't yet know how to implement the MVVM pattern—or developers who have some exposure to MVVM and want to master the techniques to apply the MVVM pattern effectively. To do that, you must have some basic knowledge of WPF and Silverlight; if you don't, I suggest you familiarize yourself with the topics of routed commands, data binding, data templates, and styling—before reading this book.

Assumptions

With a heavy focus on design patterns, software architectures, and agile techniques and methodologies, this book assumes that you have a basic understanding of how to create a WPF or Silverlight application with .NET Framework and Visual Studio. It further assumes that you have already developed an application that connects to a database, including a UI that interacts with users.

All the sample code provided in the book was created using the Visual C# language provided with .NET Framework 4. You need a solid understanding of C# to follow and use the code. The book works with both WPF and Silverlight extensively, so you should have at least a basic knowledge of these two technologies (and a firm grounding in the XAML markup language as well—the book uses some XAML sample code).

Organization of This Book

This book has been developed in such a way that each chapter focuses on a specific topic. The first chapter, "Introduction to Model View ViewModel Applications," is a general introduction to LOB applications, their components, and their structure. Chapter 2, "Design Patterns," shows a complete overview of all the well-known design patterns and architectural patterns used to develop enterprise applications, and more generally, to develop loosely-coupled components. Chapter 3, "The Domain Model," is an introduction to the domain model and Domain-Driven Design (DDD). It illustrates how to achieve DDD design goals, and how to avoid common mistakes that typically occur when building a DDD application. Chapter 4, "The Data Access Layer," concentrates on the Data Access Layer (DAL) and how you can build one by using an O/RM, such as Entity Framework and/or NHibernate. Chapter 5, "The Business Layer," focuses its attention on the design and construction of a Business Logic Layer (BLL), including in-depth coverage of business rules, business rule engines, and Service-Oriented Architecture (SOA) designs. Finally, Chapter 6, "The UI Layer with MVVM," discusses MVVM in depth, while Chapter 7, "MVVM Frameworks and Toolkits," lists available frameworks and tools that you might find useful when building LOB applications with MVVM.

Finding Your Best Starting Point in This Book

The chapters of the book cover different aspects of building an enterprise LOB application. Except for the first two chapters, which are more of a general overview of the techniques used in the book, each chapter focuses on a specific layer of a LOB application. The following table may help you determine how best to proceed if you plan to focus only on a specific layer.

If you are	Follow these steps
New to LOB applications and layered applications	Read the entire book and experiment with the solutions used as examples in each chapter.
Familiar to Design Patterns and Software architectures, but not mastered yet	Briefly skim Chapters 1 and 2 for a quick review of the core concepts. Then read the remaining chapters carefully, working to apply the principles you'll encounter in each chapter to your daily tasks.
Interested *only* in a specific layer, such as the DAL or BLL	Carefully read the specific chapter that covers the layer in which you're interested. However, to set the context, you should also skim the other chapters.
Interested only in MVVM	Read chapters 1 and 2 to fortify your knowledge about design patterns and presentation patterns, and then read chapters 6 and 7 carefully.

Conventions and Features in This Book

This book presents information using conventions designed to make the information readable and easy to follow.

In most cases, the book includes separate exercises for Visual Basic programmers and Visual C# programmers. You can skip the exercises that do not apply to your selected language.

- Boxed elements with labels such as "Note" provide additional information or alternative methods for completing a step successfully.

- Text that you should type (apart from code blocks) appears in bold.

- A plus sign (+) between two key names means that you must press those keys at the same time. For example, "Press Alt+Tab" means that you hold down the Alt key while you press the Tab key.

- A vertical bar between two or more menu items (for example, File | Close), means that you should select the first menu or menu item, then the next, and so on.

System Requirements

You will need the following hardware and software to work with the code and examples in this book:

- Any of the following operating systems: Windows XP with Service Pack 3 (except Starter Edition), Windows Vista with Service Pack 2 (except Starter Edition), Windows 7, Windows Server 2003 with Service Pack 2, Windows Server 2003 R2, Windows Server 2008 with Service Pack 2, or Windows Server 2008 R2.

- Visual Studio 2010, any edition (multiple downloads might be required if using Express Edition products).

- SQL Server 2008 Express Edition or higher (2008 or R2 release), with SQL Server Management Studio 2008 Express or higher (included with Visual Studio, Express Editions require separate download).

- 1.6 GHz or faster processor (2 GHz recommended).

- 1 GB (32-Bit) or 2 GB (64-Bit) RAM (Add 512 MB if running in a virtual machine or SQL Server Express Editions; more for advanced SQL Server editions).

- 3.5 GB of available hard disk space.

- 5400 RPM hard disk drive.

- DirectX 9 capable video card running at 1024 × 768 or higher resolution display.

- DVD-ROM drive (if installing Visual Studio from DVD).

- Internet connection to download software or chapter examples.

Depending on your Windows configuration, you might require Local Administrator rights to install or configure Visual Studio 2010 and SQL Server 2008 products.

Code Samples

Most of the chapters in this book include exercises that let you interactively try out new material learned in the main text. All sample projects, in both their pre-exercise and post-exercise formats, are available for download from this book's page on the website for Microsoft's publishing partner, O'Reilly Media:

http://oreilly.com/catalog/9780735650923/

Click the Examples link on that page. When a list of files appears, locate and download the Mvvm-Crm.zip file.

> **Note** In addition to the code samples, your system should have Visual Studio 2010 and SQL Server 2008 installed. The instructions below use SQL Server Management Studio 2008 to set up the sample database that is used with the practice examples. If available, install the latest service packs for each product.

Installing the Code Samples

To install the code samples on your computer

1. Unzip the MvvmCrm.zip file that you downloaded from *http://oreilly.com/catalog/9780735650923/*.

2. If prompted, review the displayed end user license agreement. If you accept the terms, select the accept option, and then click Next.

   > **Note** If the license agreement doesn't appear, you can access it from the same web page from which you downloaded the MvvmCrm.zip file.

Using the Code Samples

The structure of the Visual Studio solution provided with the book is divided into six different projects, in which each project composes the full source code of the related chapter in the book. The entire application then composes the CRM program, developed in WPF.

Acknowledgments

When you are the sole author of a book, you are indelibly associated with that book's merits; in fact, this is one of the reasons many people want to write a book. But even as a sole author, you aren't the only person responsible for a book becoming a reality. I want to thank all the people who have helped me to write and publish this book, because without them, it would have remained just an idea.

This is my first book. Writing it has been an amazing adventure for me, and I hope this is just the beginning of something new; something I feel is my natural bent. I wouldn't have been able to write this book without the immense help of my wonderful wife, Deborah. Writing a book requires time, and I work full time for an insurance company, so the few remaining hours of the days spent writing the book and looking for documentation (which took a full six months) were taken out of my time with her. Without such a tremendous and understanding wife, I probably wouldn't have been able to take that time. Many times, when I was close to quitting without finishing the book—due to its complexity and the sheer volume of information—she steadfastly pushed me to complete the job, just as a perfect project manager should do! Thanks, Debbie!

I also want to thank Russell Jones, my editor and primary publishing contact for this book. He is the only person who believed in me from the beginning, and he put himself on the line to get this project approved by Microsoft Press. I will always be thankful to him for that. He also did a wonderful job in helping me to complete the job on time and to organize the whole project.

Finally, I want to thank David Hill, who is both this book's technical reviewer and my mentor. David is a technical lead at Microsoft in the patterns & practices team. Having his invaluable insight while writing this book helped a great deal to refine and improve my understanding of presentation patterns in general as well as the right way to architect a Line of Business application. David is both flexible and modest. I am extremely fortunate to have had the opportunity to work with him, and fervently hope to work with him again in the future.

Thanks, guys!

Errata and Book Support

We've made every effort to ensure the accuracy of this book and its companion content. If you do find an error, please report it on our Microsoft Press site at oreilly.com:

1. Go to *http://microsoftpress.oreilly.com*.

2. In the Search box, enter the book's ISBN or title.

3. Select your book from the search results.

4. On your book's catalog page, under the cover image, you'll see a list of links.

5. Click View/Submit Errata.

You'll find additional information and services for your book on its catalog page. If you need additional support, please e-mail Microsoft Press Book Support at *mspinput@microsoft.com*.

Please note that product support for Microsoft software is not offered through the addresses above.

We Want to Hear from You

At Microsoft Press, your satisfaction is our top priority, and your feedback is our most valuable asset. Please tell us what you think of this book at:

http://www.microsoft.com/learning/booksurvey

The survey is short, and we read every one of your comments and ideas. Thanks in advance for your input!

Stay in Touch

Let's keep the conversation going! We're on Twitter at *http://twitter.com/MicrosoftPress*.

Chapter 1
Introduction to Model View ViewModel and Line of Business Applications

After completing this chapter, you will be able to:

- Identify a Line of Business application.

- Decide which is the right technology for you to develop a Line of Business application.

The Model View ViewModel Pattern

The Model View ViewModel (MVVM) pattern was introduced by John Gossman (Software Architect at Microsoft for Windows Presentation Foundation and Silverlight technologies) in 2005 on his blog. MVVM is a specialization of the Presentation Model (PM) pattern that was introduced in 2004 by Martin Fowler.

One of the main goals of the PM pattern is to separate and abstract the View—the visible user interface (UI)—from the presentation logic to make the UI testable. Additional goals might include making the presentation logic reusable for different UIs and different UI technologies, reducing the coupling between the UI and other code, and allowing UI Designers to work in a more independent manner. MVVM is a specialized interpretation of the PM pattern designed to satisfy the requirements of Windows Presentation Foundation (WPF) and Silverlight.

Structurally, an MVVM application consists primarily of three major components: the *Model*, the *View*, and the *ViewModel*.

- The Model is the entity that represents the business concept; it can be anything from a simple customer entity to a complex stock trade entity.

- The View is the graphical control or set of controls responsible for rendering the Model data on screen. A View can be a WPF window, a Silverlight page, or just an XAML data template control.

- The ViewModel is the magic behind everything. The ViewModel contains the UI logic, the commands, the events, and a reference to the Model. In MVVM, the ViewModel is not in charge of updating the data displayed in the UI—thanks to the powerful

1

data-binding engine provided by WPF and Silverlight, the ViewModel doesn't need to do that. This is because the View is an observer of the ViewModel, so as soon as the ViewModel changes, the UI updates itself. For that to happen, the ViewModel must implement the *INotifyPropertyChanged* interface and fire the *PropertyChanged* event.

Initially, only WPF was powerful enough to satisfy the MVVM pattern's requirements. In Silverlight 2, you had the option of implementing MVVM, but it was harder than implementing MVVM with WPF. Now, with Silverlight version 4, you can apply MVVM to both WPF and Silverlight in the same way, using the power of data-binding, commanding, behaviors, and data templates.

When you apply the MVVM pattern, you must take special care with the ViewModel. Because it has so many responsibilities, it's easy to create messy solutions in which you find yourself writing the same code again and again. However, when using a proper approach, the MVVM pattern can save time and helps to make your UI testable and easy to maintain. Of course, to use MVVM properly, it's mandatory that you master XAML and its UI structure. You also need to know how the binding engine of XAML works and how command objects and command behaviors *(ICommand)* and data templates are structured. Finally, to use MVVM effectively with both WPF and Silverlight, you need to know about the differences between WPF and Silverlight.

This book analyzes each component of the MVVM pattern in depth. At the end, you will create a simple MVVM Line of Business application that can be used as a template for any future MVVM application. At the same time, you'll build a small utility MVVM framework that functions as a "plug-and-play" component that you can use in your WPF or Silverlight applications to simplify writing MVVM applications. For example, the framework will provide a basic ViewModel class, a sample Message Broker, and other features required in a typical MVVM application.

Line of Business Applications

In my experience, the best way to learn a technology is by doing—building an application step by step. A Line of Business (LOB) application makes the best example for several reasons: it's suitable for the flexible UI technology found in both WPF and Silverlight; it's amenable to the MVVM pattern; and it's a common application type, so you can reuse the examples later, for real business purposes.

Note LOB applications are those that are vital to running an enterprise, such as accounting, supply chain management, or resource planning. LOB applications are usually large programs that contain a number of integrated capabilities, and tie into other applications and database management systems. They are also commonly referred to as "enterprise" applications.

A LOB application can be any business-critical application: the CRM used in the office, the account software used by the financial department to prepare the payroll, or any other type of business application that follows specific guidelines and that has a specific *common* UI style. If you think about it, such applications fit perfectly into the concept of a "template."

LOB applications are both the most requested by customers and the easiest to develop. But at the same time, they are the most difficult to develop. This is because while their *structure* is usually pretty simple and redundant, their *requirements* often change during the development process as well as during their lifetime.

Increasingly, LOB applications are gaining web interfaces, making them easy to access via browsers, easier to deploy and update, and because they enable some business scenarios that require both business partners and customers to access the same features. They're also acquiring personal application features, such as e-mail and address books.

A LOB application follows an incremental design, especially during the development process. A Scrum project management book that I read a while ago (thanks to my CTO, who has an addiction to agile techniques) mentioned that the greatest expenditures of IT departments and software houses is for *maintenance* of existing software. Usually, people involved in a software project of any type believe that the most expensive part is the *development* phase leading to the initial release, but it's only after the release that the real pain starts. For example, suppose that you create and sell an accounting application that was not originally designed to include HR payrolls. After a while, customers will ask you for this new "feature." If your design is not flexible enough to accommodate new requests and changes, you will probably lose customers and the application will fail.

A LOB application is the best fit for WPF/Silverlight and the MVVM pattern because it focuses on all the common problems that a small, medium, or large team will encounter during the various phases of the development process, and that you can solve by using these flexible technologies. Unfortunately, a book can't teach you everything, so in this book, you will not learn how to build an industrial-strength CRM application, or how to apply Scrum in your team—but you will learn how to build a LOB application that implements a small CRM using the latest Microsoft technologies.

Choosing the Right Technology

Because you can build a LOB application with either WPF or Silverlight, you'll need to analyze the project's requirements to determine which technology is most appropriate for that particular application and which tools you might want to use to build it. To answer these questions, you'll first explore how to choose between Silverlight and WPF, and then explore the tools that Microsoft currently offers for UI design and mockup. Finally, you'll move on to analyze the common graphical layout of a LOB application, and what users expect from it.

Silverlight or WPF?

Silverlight and WPF are both based on the same core technology: the Microsoft .NET Framework. In both, you build UIs using the XAML language.

WPF is the successor to Windows Forms, so it's designed to incorporate a complete set of UI controls and media elements with which you can produce rich and interactive Windows client applications. Silverlight is a cross-browser, cross-platform technology that supports rich internet applications. There is some crossover; for example, browsers can host WPF applications, and Silverlight can run out-of-the-browser on desktops, but overall, WPF is intended for Windows client applications, and Silverlight is intended for rich web applications.

The compatibility between Silverlight and WPF exists because both use the same UI description language (XAML), the same stack of UI components (although Silverlight uses only a subset of this stack), the same .NET base class library, and the CLR. The only major difference here is that Silverlight currently uses a different implementation of the .NET CLR.

Figure 1-1 displays the main differences between these two technologies.

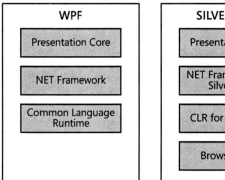
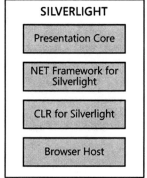

FIGURE 1-1 WPF and Silverlight architectural overview.

Because Silverlight focuses on the multi-platform, cross-browser web audience, Microsoft was constrained to keeping its runtime smaller and lighter. The takeaway here is that it's best to plan the final target of your LOB application from the beginning, because you won't find all the features of WPF available in Silverlight, and it's far more difficult to migrate from one target to the other later.

Of course, both WPF and Silverlight are improving with every release, so the hope is that we'll get a unified framework in the future, but for now, it's important to remember that the targets of these two technologies are slightly different.

Note Wintellect, in collaboration with Microsoft, has released a whitepaper at *http://
wpfslguidance.codeplex.com* that fully explains the differences between these two technologies.
The whitepaper is approximately 69 pages long. As you might expect, this book can't cover all of
the differences; therefore, it only highlights the most significant among them.

The first gap is with technologies crucial to the implementation of MVVM. Silverlight doesn't
implement routed commands, triggers, or the data template in the same way as WPF.
Therefore, to get the same (or similar) behavior, you need to implement some custom functionality in Silverlight. But first, a word of caution regarding the use of triggers in WPF and
Silverlight when you implement the MVVM pattern: they should not be heavily used because
they can easily incorporate presentation logic that can't be tested. The logic is not available
in the ViewModel but it is exposed in the View with the trigger.

Silverlight 4 ships with a rich set of controls, styles, and templates, one of which is a nice
LOB ASP.NET Model View Contoller (MVC) website template. In contrast, WPF ships with a
smaller and lighter control toolbox.

So, which should you use—Silverlight or WPF? The answer is: make your choice based on
the type of application you're building and the most common target of your application. For
example, if you're going to develop a LOB application for a financial department that will
not be used outside the customer's company, WPF is the right technology for you. On the
other hand, if you need to develop a CRM application that will be used by customers and
managers who might have different devices, then it makes sense to host the application in a
browser; thus, Silverlight is the right technology.

You can easily build two UI layers if you use the MVVM pattern correctly: one layer for WPF,
and one layer for Silverlight. Right now, many developers follow this two-UI–layer approach.

The final target and purposes of your application are the keys that should determine your
choice of which technology to use. Don't worry about differences in the control set or the UI
at this point; Microsoft has released a set of designer tools (Microsoft Expression Studio) that
can handle all the design process needs for both WPF and Silverlight.

Microsoft's UI-Building Tools

The biggest problem for developers who want to move to WPF or Silverlight is the learning
curve. These two technologies use a new UI language specification called XAML, which is
nothing more than a declarative markup language like HTML or XML. Of course, it's not easy
to use this language to build graphical layouts when you don't know how the XAML rendering engine works. Similarly, it's not easy to implement full designer support for a WYSIWYG
approach. XAML is a very flexible markup language with few limitations. For example, you
can place a *DataGrid* into a Button—even though that might make no sense in terms of
usability. Such flexibility can drive graphical engines crazy.

To help solve such problems, Microsoft has released a package of graphical tools called Expression Studio. The latest version is Expression Studio 4, which must be bought separately (you can also buy each individual tool available in the Expression package separately). This full "Office application set for WPF/Silverlight designers" covers the entire design process of an XAML application, from initial UI mockup to all the design elements included in the final product. Some of the tools in Expression Studio, such as Expression Web, are specifically for web designers. Expression Blend, aimed at user interface designers, separates not only the procedural code from the markup, but also separates design tasks from development tasks, letting developers focus on writing business code while leaving designers free to design functional UI without having to know C#, or Visual Basic, or any other .NET Language. MVVM is key to this design/development collaboration process. In fact, Expression Blend ships with a specific namespace that developers can use to create a mockup ViewModel for the designers. Designers can then bind the View to this mirror of the final ViewModel and continue developing the UI layer.

You can download Expression Studio from *http://www.microsoft.com/expression/* in a 60-day trial version, purchase it online, or get it through an MSDN subscription.

Expression Blend

For a WPF/Silverlight designer, Expression Blend is the primary Expression Suite product. Its project files are completely compatible with Microsoft Visual Studio. You (or a designer) can work on a project in Expression Blend, and then later open the project in Visual Studio, and vice versa. This bi-directional compatibility makes it easy to use Expression Blend to design the template and the controls of your LOB application, and then move to Visual Studio to write your .NET code. Despite this convenience, moving back and forth between Expression Blend and Visual Studio is not mandatory, because Expression Blend can render XAML and build C# and Visual Basic solutions just like Visual Studio.

Using Expression Blend, you can design an XAML user interface, create a control library for Silverlight, or WPF, or simply design and apply custom styles to your XAML application. One truly powerful Expression Blend feature is its ability to create a design-time data template. This capability means that a graphic designer doesn't need a "real" database or data files to represent a realistic result in the designer; Expression Blend lets you easily set up a data template, or you can ask Expression Blend to generate one. The final result appears in the Integrated Development Environment (IDE) and looks just like the results you would get using real data.

Expression Blend 4, the latest version, has full design-time support for WPF and Silverlight, and makes the designer's job much easier. In addition, Expression Blend also has a specific Behaviors SDK that adds design-time support for the MVVM pattern. This feature makes Expression Blend the UI designer's tool of choice for applications involving MVVM.

Finally, just to mention a couple more new features in the latest version of Expression Blend, you can easily build and emulate applications for the new mobile Windows Phone 7 platform; create cool transitions and animations for your Silverlight or WPF applications; or create, animate, and deploy dynamic user interface mockups.

Figure 1-2 shows a populated data template in Expression Blend.

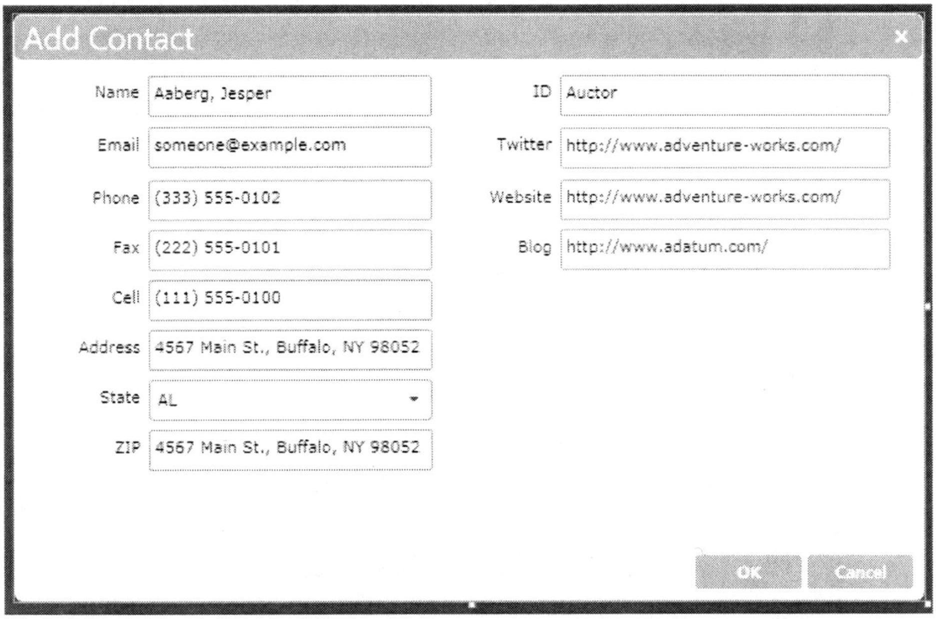

FIGURE 1-2 Microsoft Expression Blend data template.

Figure 1-2 uses a simple data template to display the state of the ViewModel and its data template at design time. The code to do that is pretty simple. It uses data binding to map the values between the UI and the ViewModel, as shown in the following:

```
<Grid x:Name="LayoutRoot" d:DataContext="{d:DesignData/SampleData/
ContactsViewModelSampleData.xaml}">
  <!--
    omitted code
  -->
      <data:DataGridTextColumn Binding="{Binding Name}" Header="NAME" Width="0.25*"/>
      <data:DataGridTextColumn Binding="{Binding Email}" Header="EMAIL" Width="0.35*"/>
  <!--
    omitted code
  -->
      <i:InvokeCommandAction Command="{Binding AddContactCommand}"/>
  </Grid>
```

Microsoft Sketchflow

Microsoft SketchFlow is a UI mockup feature that ships with Expression Blend. SketchFlow lets you quickly design a mockup of the user interface and add some minimal interaction between the sketches.

One critical step in delivering a new application is to get feedback from the customer as soon as possible—even before the UI development process starts. Using Sketchflow, you can provide a quick mockup of your application, and even give it to end users so they can see and provide feedback for modifications. You can publish SketchFlow mockups to a Silverlight or WPF player where users can interact with them, adding notes and drawings to capture feedback. By using SketchFlow to support early user testing, you don't need to design a full user interface before getting feedback from the customer.

Sketchflow is fully integrated with Expression Blend. It ships with a custom set of controls that are really nothing more than classic XAML controls with a custom theme. Figure 1-3 displays the main Microsoft Sketchflow window.

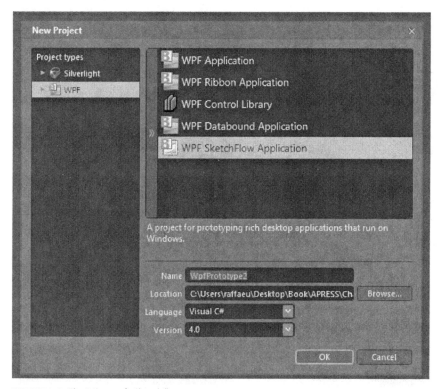

FIGURE 1-3 The Microsoft Sketchflow start page.

Using Sketchflow in collaboration with Expression Blend, you can bind mockup data to a dummy ViewModel so that when you apply the MVVM pattern in this process the UI design can evolve independently from the business logic (for example, using SketchFlow to tweak the UI design). Later, you can switch out the dummy ViewModel.

Figure 1-4 displays the final result of a mockup built using Sketchflow.

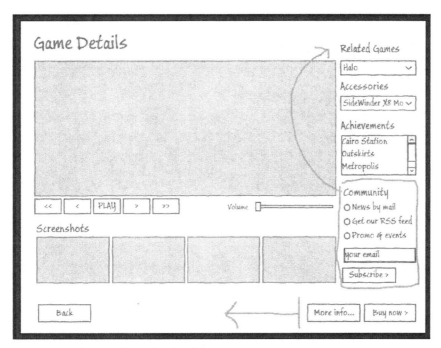

FIGURE 1-4 A final mockup using Sketchflow.

Composition of a LOB User Interface

In large development shops, by using the Expression Suite and Visual Studio products, you can easily divide your application among two different teams without affecting productivity; one team will use the Expression tools to mockup and develop the user interface, while the other team will focus on implementing core features and activating the UI. MVVM makes this clean separation possible because it gives you the power to make the UI only loosely coupled to the UI business logic contained in the ViewModel. Of course, this concept doesn't mean that you *must* divide your team into Designers versus Developers if you plan to adopt the MVVM pattern.

One fundamental concept that you need to understand to build a successful LOB application or any other application that involves user interfaces is that *users see only UI*. End users don't know (and don't care) that your application uses the latest version of SQL Server, or that submitting an order involves interacting with a NASA web service. The user interacts only with the user interface. Therefore, it's important to stay focused on a few concepts that will render the UI properly and that will help prevent users from becoming lost in your applications. Before starting to define each part of a LOB user interface, it's worth looking at a very successful Microsoft example that represents a classic LOB application: Microsoft Dynamics, shown in Figure 1-5.

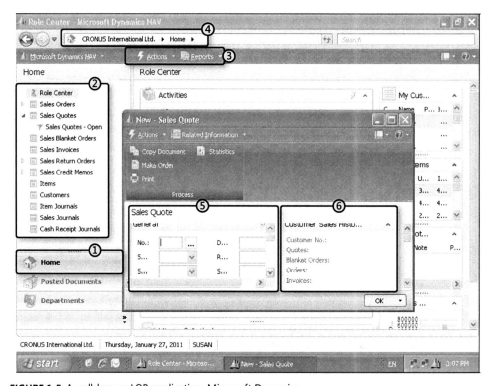

FIGURE 1-5 A well-known LOB application, Microsoft Dynamics.

Figure 1-5 contains several highlighted items with numbered callouts, which are addressed in the paragraphs that follow.

It's very common for a LOB application to use a *navigation pane* (area 1 in Figure 1-5). You can build a navigation pane easily with a XAML tab control and some styles. You'll probably recognize this navigation pane as the classic navigation scheme used in programs such as Microsoft Outlook. The goal of a navigation pane is to group, or gather, functionality into one place. As you can see from Figure 1-5, Dynamics groups the various major sections of the application into high-level concepts such as Finance, Inventory, and so on. This way, users can easily access any section of the LOB application. When a user clicks one of the high-level concepts, the section for that concept is loaded into a more detailed View at the top of the navigation pane (area 2).

At the top of the application you'll see both a *Toolbar* (area 3) and a *Menubar* (area 4). The Menubar resides at the top of the application and should provide access to all the available commands. The toolbar is a graphical shortcut to the most-used commands. The Toolbar should be context-sensitive; for example, it should enable the Save button only when the current View has changes and needs to be saved.

Note Menus should be context-sensitive as well, but because menu sub-items are not visible as users work within the UI, menu context sensitivity is less apparent than that of toolbars.

Note In many modern applications, such as Office 2010, the toolbar and menu bar are being replaced by a combination of the two, called a Ribbon. You'll see more about the Ribbon later in this chapter.

The *current view* (areas 5 and 6) displays data that the user is currently working with in the application. In this case Dynamics uses a Multiple Document Interface (MDI) approach, where each open View has a separate window. Another possible approach is to use tabs for each View; this is the default style adopted by Visual Studio, for example.

The following section provides a more detailed explanation of each major area, and discusses some best practices for building useful LOB application UIs.

The Menubar

The Menubar is the menu at the top of any application. It is the topmost container, and it should contain all the available commands in the application, divided into related sections. The Menubar should also include such common sections, such as File, Edit, and Help.

The Menubar is a critical LOB application component, so your Menubars should adhere to some specific design policies; otherwise, they will lose their potential.

Some common Menubar rules are as follows:

- Whenever possible, include an underline (_) character in each item's text. In .NET, the underline defines that item's access key. Adding the underlines lets users browse through the menus using the Alt key in conjunction with the access key.
- Respect common shortcut key combinations. For example, in Windows the Save command is typically represented by the shortcut Ctrl+S.
- Add an icon that represents each command's context. The image should be clear and understandable, and the size of the image must be 16 × 16 pixels. Figure 1-6 shows an example of a menu with icon images.

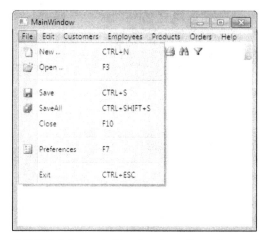

FIGURE 1-6 A sample Menubar that reflects the standard guidelines.

The Toolbar

The Toolbar is a graphical control that is typically positioned immediately below the Menubar. The common characteristic of a Toolbar (as opposed to a Menubar), is that it provides users with visual controls rather than simple labels. Usually the Toolbar contains a set of buttons (and sometimes other controls) each of which has a clear and distinguishable image that suggests what that button's function is. The normal size for a Toolbar icon is 22 × 22 pixels or, at most, 24 × 24 pixels. You might also consider using classic 16-pixel images, but in my opinion they are too small for a normal Toolbar.

You can include text labels on your Toolbar buttons, but try to avoid this when possible. Usually, users have only the image to indicate the function of a Toolbar button, so the clearer and more self-explanatory your images are, the more useful the Toolbar will be.

Because the Toolbar supports the same (or fewer) commands that are already available in the Menubar, using the MVVM approach, you might wish to use the same ViewModel for both controls or to provide a collection of commands for each ViewModel and build a *DataTemplate* to render them. You'll see more about how to do that in the next chapters. You could theoretically accomplish this with the Ribbon control provided for WPF and Silverlight, but the complexity of the UI and the logic behind it will require a specific PM dedicated to the Ribbon control.

The Tooltip (and Its Abuse)

Despite the best design intentions, sometimes circumstances force you to position too many controls in one area, or to place images and controls such that even the most expert user can easily become lost. When the user interface is not completely clear, you should provide users with dynamic feedback from the UI to help them make the best decisions.

One way to provide such feedback is through the Tooltip control. This is a little window that appears when users hover their mouse over a specific control. The purpose of the Tooltip is to provide an immediate description of the selected control. That's it, nothing more, and nothing less. So, for example, if a user hovers the mouse over a Toolbar button with an image of a floppy disk, common sense suggests that the Tooltip text for that image should read something like: "*Save. Save the current record.*" This is a clear and immediate description, but it is not too complex.

While Tooltips can be helpful, there is one problem I often see when working with WPF/ Silverlight developers; because XAML has few limits, it's easy to add a Tooltip to a Datagrid or any other control. But overusing Tooltips defeats their purpose. The key is to remember that the goal of a Tooltip is simply to provide temporary and transient help by means of a brief description of the current control. If you need to extend the *behavior* of that control, consider adopting a different solution. For example, WPF has a nice tag called *Popup*, where you can store any control and use it to show more information using the pop-up concept.

Because of its powerful render template, Tooltips can be easily misunderstood and used improperly. When you plan to write a tooltip for a specific control (textbox, button, label, and so forth), remember that the Tooltip will stay on the screen for just a few seconds. Therefore, it should contain only a few words that describe its associated control. If you determine that your Tooltip needs more than few words to describe the control, it means that there are two problems:

- The control that needs the Tooltip is placed in the wrong View or might not be clear at all; consider using a label to identify this control to simplify (or eliminate) the Tooltip.

- The operation done by that control is too complex to describe easily. In such cases, you might need a more detailed help solution, or you might consider splitting the operation into different controls, using a Wizard or a validation icon to identify potential errors caused by the operation.

- As with the Toolbar and the Menubar, a good approach to creating uniform Tooltips is to create a specific *DataTemplate* stored in a common dictionary. By using this approach, every control in your application that uses a Tooltip can use the same style. I want to stress here that a Tooltip is just a UI artifact that a designer can choose to support or not support; it doesn't define any UI logic, so it doesn't need to be represented in the ViewModel.

Notifications and Alerts

Communication with users is paramount in UI construction. One common need for communication is when you want to notify users that entered or selected data is invalid, or that they're attempting to perform an invalid operation. At the same time, you want to make your user interface minimally invasive and reduce frustration as much as possible. As an example, if every time a user clicks the Save button your UI asks for confirmation—such as the all-too-familiar prompt *"Are you sure you want to save?"*—after only a few hours using the application, the user will be really frustrated.

But you also need to be sure that users don't execute invalid or inappropriate commands, or enter invalid data. Typically, you do this by adding some validation logic to the user interface.

Remember though, that in almost every case, it's far more useful to disable invalid actions in advance. As an example (and as you'll see later), when using the MVVM approach it's better to set the *CanExecute* context of a button to *false*, rather than letting users click it, and then showing them a frustrating *MessageBox* notification.

WPF and Silverlight offer various ways to communicate with the user. Historically, developers have used modal dialog boxes, which pop up and capture all application input until dismissed. It is called a "dialog box" because it establishes a dialog between the UI and the user. Dialogs can be unidirectional (notifying users about an error, for example), or bidirectional (users are asked to confirm or cancel an operation).

The dialog approach is easy to implement but very invasive for users. Displaying a dialog forces users to click a button—such as "Yes" or "No." Because dialogs capture all application input, until the user responds, the entire UI simply freezes. Dialogs are appropriate when you need a confirmation, such as when a user tries to delete a record, but in most other cases you should use a different approach.

The MVVM pattern makes it more difficult to implement the dialog approach because the ViewModel doesn't know anything about the View, so it doesn't know how to interact with it. An easy solution to this problem is the *mediator pattern*. You'll analyze this pattern in more depth in Chapter 6, "The UI Layer with MVVM."

> **Note** The Mediator is a behavioral design pattern that provides a central hub to guide interactions between many objects. When you analyze the composite UI framework built by the Microsoft patterns & practices team in Chapter 7, "MVVM Frameworks and Toolkits," you will see that there are also better ways to accomplish this task.

Another interesting approach that fits well into the MVVM pattern is using validators and the *IDataErrorInfo* interface applied to the ViewModel. For example, when you require a specific data format in a control, you can use a validation notification, which in WPF and Silverlight is both easy and clean. If a user has entered incorrect data into a control, you can easily highlight that control and display an error message. Unlike dialogs, such messages do not require confirmation and do not freeze the UI. When validation errors occur, users can continue to work with the UI, but they won't be able to submit the data until it's fixed. Figure 1-7 shows an example of a Silverlight LOB application that validates data before sending it to the server.

FIGURE 1-7 Custom data validation using Silverlight 4.

The key point here is that you need to choose appropriate methods for handling errors and confirmations for which you want to force users to respond, as opposed to those that provide advice or other information, for which you don't need to force users to respond. For the latter, you can consider a less invasive approach.

The Ribbon Bar

Since the Microsoft Office 2007 products were introduced a few years ago, Windows users have begun to get comfortable with a new custom control known as the "Ribbon." The Ribbon is a set of tools that includes the functionality of both a Menubar and a Toolbar, wrapped into a more modern approach. The Ribbon got its name as the result of a meeting of the Outlook 2003 team, at which they decided to implement this new control for the first time. The idea was to implement something similar to a medieval scroll, where a long strip of paper can be scrolled using one of the two spindles. Using this concept, the team introduced the concept of Tabs and Groups in the existing Ribbon control.

The purpose of the Ribbon is to reduce the number of menus floating around your application. In fact if you plan to introduce a Ribbon bar in your application, you will no longer need a Toolbar or Menubar, because the Ribbon subsumes those functions. Ribbons have some very restrictive design constraints, so if you plan to use one, you should follow the design policies suggested by Microsoft, which are available here: *http://msdn.microsoft.com/en-us/library/cc872782.aspx.*

Note During the writing of this book, Microsoft released the final version of the Ribbon control for WPF 4, compiled in .NET 3.5 SP1, with full support for the MVVM pattern.

The Ribbon control has been released in beta for WPF 3.5 (and works with WPF 4) but it's not available for Silverlight. You might want to consider a third-party solution if you plan to use a Ribbon in a Silverlight application.

The WPF Ribbon bar was designed to work with MVVM; it has native support for routed commands and data binding, and it's also easy to customize. The Ribbon control's structure, which uses regions and groups, is probably the best match so far for an MVVM-rich menu control.

Figure 1-8 shows the main structure of a Ribbon bar using the Office 2007 style.

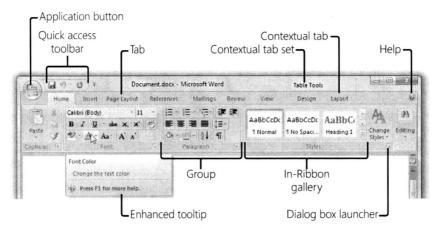

FIGURE 1-8 The Microsoft WPF Ribbon bar (from MSDN).

Before deciding if a Ribbon is a good fit for your application, be aware that the effort you need to construct a usable Ribbon is greater than that needed to create a simple Menubar or a Toolbar. Therefore, here are some things you should consider:

- **Is your application complex?** If you are building a simple UI, consider using a simple menu system rather than a Ribbon bar.

- **Do your users have problems finding and executing the right commands?** The Ribbon, if properly designed, might help ameliorate such usability problems.

- **Do you have space constraints?** Rendering a Ribbon requires significant screen space, so if you are planning to develop an application with small windows that doesn't use a Tabbed/MDI concept, the Ribbon is probably not for you.

General Style and Control Considerations

Looking backward through this chapter, you've seen that LOB application UIs have some common characteristics based on specific UI controls and specific techniques that render the controls and the views properly.

Using common styles throughout your application is critical in LOB applications—especially when you work with a flexible technology such as WPF/Silverlight.

Consider the concept of a font, which includes the font family, font face, font size, colors, and more. In most LOB applications, you should strive to minimize font use—in fact, it's best to use only one font face. Within that single font face, you can adjust the weight, size, and decorations, so one font is flexible and can meet many needs. You should avoid mixing many different fonts in the same application.

Second, and very important for most customers, is the color scheme. For this aspect of your application you need to consider two things. First, are you developing an application for a specific customer? If so, you should try to apply the company's colors to your application— or at least you should try to keep the same colors and styles as their previous application, if there was one. Such continuity helps users avoid becoming lost within the new interface. Second, are you developing the application as a software suite? Emulating existing suite applications can be a good idea. For example, the Office package uses a successful combination of colors. Emulating Office styles in XAML is possible, and it makes your application look professional, while also making it familiar and easy to understand, because most customers have already worked with Office. That familiarity can transfer to your new UI.

Finally, remember that one aspect of being effective in XAML is based on *DataTemplates* and styles. Don't waste your time creating dictionaries and styles for each view by doing massive copy and paste operations. Remember that you can use a dictionary from a different assembly and load styles on the fly. Working in this way, you can easily build an application with custom themes and deploy a specific theme for a specific customer without the need to change the entire application code. Also remember to be careful not to duplicate style and layout in multiple places; if you centralize these aspects using data templates and styles, you can guarantee more consistency in your application UI.

Note Microsoft has released a series of nice templates that customize the common controls for WPF. The Silverlight team has also released a nice set of templates for the Silverlight Business application. You can get the WPF and Silverlight Control themes from *http://wpfthemes.codeplex. com*. If you plan to use the Silverlight 4 LOB application template, you can get some themes from *http://www.microsoft.com/downloads/en/details.aspx?FamilyID=e9da0eb8-f31b-4490-85b8- 92c2f807df9e&displaylang=en*.

Separation of Concerns

In informatics, the term Separation of Concerns (SoC) refers to the process of separating pieces of code so that they overlap in functionality as little as possible. The main concept here is that you want to make an application composed of *layers*.

SoC is a key software engineering principle that states that a given problem involves different kinds of concerns, which should be identified and separated to cope with complexity and to achieve required engineering quality factors such as robustness, adaptability, maintainability, and reusability.

You can apply the principle in various ways. The most common way of separating concerns is to divide the layers by functionality. Typically, a LOB application will have a *UI layer*, the layer that composes the graphic interface; a *Domain Layer*, the layer that represents business entities (such as a Customer, an Order, and so on); a *Business Layer*, which is in charge of encapsulating all the business logic of the application; and a *Data Access Layer*, the layer in charge of persisting and retrieving data.

All programming paradigms aid developers in the process of improving SoC. For example, object-oriented programming languages such as Delphi, C++, Java, and C# separate concerns into objects; a design pattern such as MVC can separate content from presentation, and data-processing (model) from content. Service-oriented design can separate concerns into services. Procedural programming languages such as C and Pascal can separate concerns into procedures. Aspect-oriented programming languages can separate concerns into aspects and objects.

SoC is an important design principle in many other areas, as well, such as urban planning, architecture, and information design. The goal is to design systems so that functions can be optimized independently of other functions, such that failure of one function does not cause other functions to fail, and in general to make it easier to understand, design, and manage complex interdependent systems. Common examples include using corridors to connect rooms rather than having rooms open directly into each other, and keeping the stove on one circuit, and the lights on another.

A Little Taste of History

In 1974, Edsger W. Dijkstra, a Dutch computer scientist, wrote a paper called "On the role of scientific thought," which was the first paper that discussed the concept of SoC. In his paper, Mr. Dijkstra mentioned that:

> ...the separation of concerns, [is] the only available technique for effective ordering of one's thoughts, that I know of.

In 1989, Chris Reade wrote the book *Elements of Functional Programming*, in which he also mentions SoC:

> The programmer has to do several things at the same time, namely, 1. Describe what is to be computed; 2. Organize the computation sequencing into small steps; 3. Organize memory management during the computation.

Moving forward, in the years 1990–2000 (I am not going to bother you with dates...), Martin Fowler and Eric Evans started to talk about design patterns related to contextual design, leading directly to the modern concept of SoC.

Both authors, but especially Martin Fowler, began naming patterns, discussing concepts and patterns such as Domain-Driven Design, Inversion of Control, Unit of Work, and many other agile approaches to make applications that are layered, testable, and maintainable. Shortly thereafter, large companies and programming communities started to implement frameworks or application blocks that facilitated SoC in applications and worked with common programming languages such as .NET, Java, and C.

You'll see all these patterns and techniques in this book and apply them to a real-world problem.

Layers, Tiers, and Services

Using UI patterns such as MVVM forces you to divide application code into different layers. That's good, because it helps keep the application testable and flexible. Commonly, such blocks are called *layers*. Sometimes a set of layers have a specific interaction (see the MVVM pattern), and they compose a *tier*, such as the client tier in an MVVM application.

Figure 1-9 displays a conceptual sketch of the difference between layers and tiers.

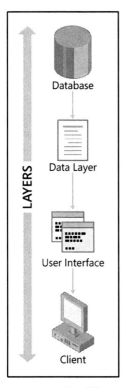
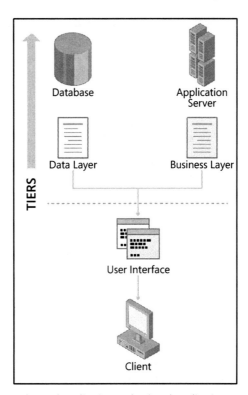

FIGURE 1-9 The difference between a layered application and a tiered application.

In a common three-tier application such as an MVVM application (UI, business logic, and database), you usually have two/three layers per tier and two tiers. The tiers are the client application and the remote database (physically separated), and the layers for the client tier might be the UI and the Presentation, while for the Business tier, they might be the Business Layer and the Data Access Layer.

When the application starts to be more complex or its distribution starts to increase, you should consider using the service-oriented application (SOA) approach. For example, in Silverlight you can't recycle the binaries of the Domain Layer or the data layer because they are not usually compiled for the Silverlight CLR. The solution in this case is to use SOA through WCF RIA Services. These services are proxies built into WCF, with which you can share the code exposed in a class library such as the domain layer, compiled for the normal NET CLR, with the Silverlight CLR. Of course, if you plan to move to SOA, you should keep in mind other problems that you might encounter, such as concurrency, transactions, service availability, and more.

History of the Service Layer

The term "Service Layer" was coined by Martin Fowler, one of the most famous software architects, who said:

> A Service Layer defines an application's boundary [Alistair Cockburn's application boundary pattern—also known as Cockburn PloP] and its set of available operations from the perspective of interfacing client layers. It encapsulates the application's business logic, controlling transactions and coordinating responses in the implementation of its operations.

If you plan to move to a Service Layer and to SOA architecture, you need to keep a lot of other architectural considerations in mind. For example, when using the Entity Framework and RIA Services, the effort required to move to an SOA solution is not large, but SOA forces you to think through some additional considerations.

SOA is complex. Microsoft technologies such as WCF and the RIA services for Silverlight can help, but unfortunately when you actually start to use SOA, you'll need to consider additional possible problems such as concurrency, transactions, and availability. You'll need to tackle each of these carefully.

 Note   The Data Transfer Object will be covered in the Chapter 3, "The Domain Model."

The Business Layer contains the "business logic" of your application. For now it's enough to know that the business logic must reside there; you'll see later how complex this layer can become. In fact, it's usually composed of two layers: one on the client side, and one on the server side. In the example LOB application for this book, the Business Layer will contain entity classes such as *Customers* and *Orders*, and business logic such as workflows and validation.

Finally the Data Access Layer is in charge of communicating with the repository—the data store, not the "repository pattern," which you'll read more about in Chapter 2, "Design Patterns." Of course, the data store can be a common database, a service, a simple text file or anything else able to store data. Usually you don't have this layer if you use an object relational mapper (O/RM) because that becomes your Data Layer. Of course, you might need to extend or expand the O/RM; if so, you will keep such extensions in the Data Layer. If everything were designed this neatly, it wouldn't be so complex to be a software architect.

You'll start by analyzing each layer in more detail to see the complexities of a "well done" layered application.

First, you have the UI, which can implement one of the following UI Patterns: MVC, MVP (Model View Presenter), or MVVM. I've purposely skipped the lesser-known patterns; it's enough to focus on just these three. Because the Presentation Layer will contain the Views (windows, widgets, and so on), the orchestration (presenter, controller, or ViewModel), and the resources, you'll probably end up with three sublayers similar to the structure in Figure 1-10.

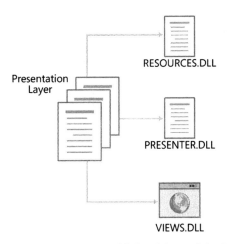

RESOURCES.DLL

Presentation
Layer

PRESENTER.DLL

VIEWS.DLL

FIGURE 1-10 One possible breakdown of the Presentation Layer.

You can imagine these three layers in Visual Studio as three different class library projects. Using this approach, you can assign each layer to a different developer, but this depends on the size of the project and on the size of the layers. Also, if you need to update just one of them, because they are loosely coupled you won't need to upgrade the entire UI layer—only the one affected by the changes. As you saw in the section about Expression Blend, you can now provide designers with a fake XAML ViewModel, allowing them to build the UI while letting developers move forward on the ViewModel assembly. If instead, the Views and the ViewModels were stored in the same assembly (the same Visual Studio Project), accomplishing this task would be difficult.

The Business Layer is a more complex concept. If you follow the Domain-Driven Design approach used in this book, you should represent the "business" in the form of classes. For example, you would have a *Customer* class that has a collection of classes such as *Address*, and so on. The end result is a class structure called a *Graph* or *Model*.

At this point, you might be thinking, "Where can I write the C# code that will allow me to add an order for a specific user?" This is a common and pretty simple "business rule," typical of a Business Layer. Usually, you'd include all such rules in a separated layer that we will call the "Service" Layer (or better, "Business Service" Layer) that should not be confused with the SOA approach.

Using this technique lets you take advantage of a third-party framework, such as Windows Workflow, to execute business rules against the domain. Of course, you can dispatch such rules using the SOA approach, but at this point the architectural considerations become more complex.

Finally, the Data Layer, which typically is not the repository itself, but the component in charge of exchanging the data between the domain and the repository. For example, if you want to create a collection of *Customer* classes using the *Customer* table in the database as a source, you would use the Data Layer to do that.

Of course, this task can be the most expensive in terms of resources, because you need to map each entity against the corresponding data in the database. You will also need to provide the mappings for commands, such as Save, Update, and so on. You will also need to maintain a blueprint of the mapping process; otherwise, when changes occur in the database, your Data Layer won't reflect this change.

Doing all this is far easier if you use an O/RM. In this book, you'll see what an O/RM is and how you can use it to map a domain entity against a database.

Summary

The MVVM pattern was introduced by Microsoft a couple of years ago to satisfy the demand for a Separated Presentation pattern specifically intended for use with WPF and Silverlight. The MVVM pattern is the best presentation pattern available for WPF and Silverlight because it's able to take advantage of specific built-in features of Silverlight and WPF, such as data binding, commands, behaviors, and so on.

LOB applications, often called "enterprise" applications, are those that have been identified as critical to the business. If you plan to write a robust and maintainable LOB application using WPF or Silverlight, it's mandatory that you implement the MVVM pattern, and it's also mandatory that you follow some UI guidelines specific to LOB applications.

The term Separation of Concerns refers to the process of separating code so that overlaps in functionality with other code occur as little as possible. The main concept here is that you want to make an application composed of *modules*, also known as *layers*. Using this approach, you can create testable and flexible applications that different teams can develop in parallel.

Chapter 2
Design Patterns

After completing this chapter, you will be able to:

- Apply the appropriate design pattern for a specific problem.
- Distinguish between the three major presentation patterns.
- Apply Inversion of Control and DSL.

An Overview of Design Patterns

Writing a computer application is a complex task—writing one that is flexible and that can be efficiently maintained is even more complex. If you are a senior developer or a software architect, you might already know that arguably the most difficult task is figuring out how to write the code only once, recycling it as much as you can to save time and make your applications easier to maintain.

As the Pirelli Company famously said about its tires, *"Power is nothing without control,"* and in this case, control is very important. When writing code, you first need to consider the likelihood that you will not be the only person working on that project or application. Second, the application might require maintenance and modification in the future. And finally—again—it's preferable to write code only once.

If you are a senior developer or a software architect, you have probably already experienced many problems during your career. In fact, you might have a common solution for a common problem that you recycle in every application when you encounter that specific problem. This type of solution—using similar code to solve similar problems—is called a *pattern*, or typically, a *design pattern*. A design pattern is a common solution for a common problem that has already been identified and tested. From the outset, let me say that this definition doesn't mean that every design pattern is the same; instead, the pattern is a tested approach to solving a common problem. In other words, it's a guideline that must be adjusted depending on the context, not used in a single, non-changing syntax.

This book uses a number of design patterns, some of which you might be familiar with, others might be completely new. For example, the Model View ViewModel (MVVM) is a user interface (UI) design pattern. Of course, design patterns are used for more than just building UIs; there are design patterns for the domain, for the UI, and for typical common problems. You won't explore each design pattern in depth in this book, because that's not the main purpose; however, it's worth looking at some of the common available design patterns to see how they might apply to the sample Line of Business (LOB) application.

A Little Taste of History

Design patterns were originally introduced by Christopher Alexander in 1977 as a common solution for a common problem in the field of construction architecture. Later, at the end of the 1980s, Kent Beck and Ward Cunningham began to apply patterns in the field of the computer science.

The first important book on design patterns for developers was *Design Patterns: Elements of Reusable Object-Oriented Software* (Addison-Wesley, 1995; ISBN: 0-20163-361-2). This well-known work was written by four software architects—the "Gang of Four" (GOF)—Erich Gamma, Richard Helm, Ralph Johnson, and John Vlissides. I highly recommend it as a fundamental book for any developer.

In 2002, Martin Fowler wrote a more advanced version of this book, *Patterns of Enterprise Application Architecture* (Addison-Wesley Professional, 2002; ISBN: 0-32112-742-0. Commonly known as "PoEAA," this book discussed architectural problems not originally covered by the GOF. In my opinion, this is another milestone of computer science literature, and again, I heartily recommend it.

Note   To analyze the topic of design patterns in more depth, go to *http://msdn.microsoft.com/ en-us/practices/default.aspx*. This page was created by Microsoft's patterns & practices team, which analyzes the architectural aspects of Microsoft technologies.

Classifying Design Patterns

The basic design patterns implemented in 1977 are divided into three major categories: *creational*, *structural*, and *behavioral*, each of which has a specific role. In addition, you can find patterns specific to UI, and advanced patterns for architectural problems. These patterns are members of a new classification, also known as the *architectural design patterns classification*.

The creational patterns are specific to solving problems related to object creation. The structural patterns deal with the composition of classes or objects, and the behavioral patterns are concerned with designing the way objects communicate or interact. These are also collectively known as Gang of Four patterns, because they were introduced in the aforementioned GOF book.

Creational Patterns

The following table presents patterns that were designed to solve problems related to the creational process of objects and classes.

Name	Description	Example
Abstract Factory	Provides a method for creating objects or classes that are related or dependent, without specifying the concrete class.	*Factory.CreateProductA();* *Factory.CreateProductB();*
Factory Method	Defines an interface for creating an object, but lets subclasses decide which class to instantiate.	*FactoryA.Create();* *FactoryB.Create();*
Builder	Separates the construction of a complex object from its representation so that the same construction process can create different representations.	*Builder.BuildPartA();* *Builder.BuildPartB();* *Build.GetFinalProduct();*
Prototype	Specifies the kind of objects to create using a prototypical instance, and creates new objects by copying this prototype.	*Product = Prototype.Clone();*
Singleton	Ensures a class has only one instance and provides a global point of access to it.	*Singleton.DoSomething();*

Structural Patterns

The next table introduces patterns that were designed to solve problems related to the composition of an object or class.

Name	Description	Example
Adapter	Converts the interface of a class into another interface that clients expect.	*Target obj = new Adapter();* *obj.DoSomething();*
Bridge	Decouples an abstraction from its implementation so that the two can vary independently.	*Var obj = new ConcreteA();* *obj.DoSomething();* *obj = new ConcreteB();* *obj.DoSomething();*
Composite	Composes objects into tree structures to represent part-whole hierarchies.	*Composite.Add(objA);* *Composite.Add(objB);*
Decorator	Attaches additional responsibilities to an object dynamically.	*obj.SetDecorator(decA);* *obj.DoDecoration();* *obj.SetDecorator(decB);* *obj.DoDecoration();*
Facade	Provides a unified interface to a set of interfaces in a subsystem.	*Façade.MethodFromObjA();* *Façade.MethodFromObjB();*
Flyweight	Uses sharing to support large numbers of fine-grained objects efficiently.	*A = FWFactory.GetFW("A");* *B = FWFactory.GetFW("B");*
Proxy	Provides a surrogate or placeholder for another object to control access to it.	*var proxy = new Proxy();* *proxy.RequestChannel();*

Behavioral Patterns

The table that follows describes patterns that were designed to solve problems related to the behavior and interaction between objects or classes.

Name	Description	Example
Chain of Response	Avoids coupling the sender of a request to its receiver by giving more than one object a chance to handle the request.	*Employee.SetSupervisor(Manager);* *Manager.SetSupervisor(Director);* *Employee.Execute();*
Command	Encapsulates a request as an object and supports undoable operations.	*Command.DoSomething();* *Command.Redo();* *Command.Undo();*
Interpreter	Given a language, defines a representation for its grammar.	*Vocabulary.Add(expressionA);* *Vocabulary.Add(expressionB);* *Vocabulary.Translate();*
Mediator	Defines an object that encapsulates how a set of objects interact.	*Mediator.Add(ObjA);* *Mediator.Add(ObjB);* *ObjA.Send("ObjB", Message");*
Memento	Without violating encapsulation, captures and externalizes an object's internal state so that the object can be restored to this state later.	*ObjA.Name = "ObjA";* *Memento.Save(ObjA);* *Memento.Restore(ObjA);*
Observer	Defines a one-to-many dependency between objects so that when one object changes state, all its dependents are notified and updated automatically.	*Observer.Attach(ObjA);* *Observer.Attach(ObjB);* *Observer.ChangeSomething();* *Observer.Notify();*
State	Allows an object to alter its behavior when its internal state changes. The object will appear to change its class.	*Context.Add(ObjA);* *ObjA.ChangeState("A);* *ObjA.ChangeState("B");*
Strategy	Defines a family of algorithms, encapsulates each one, and makes them interchangeable. Using Strategy, the algorithm can vary independently from clients that use it.	*List.Add(ObjA);* *List.Add(ObjB);* *List.SortStrategy(Ascending);* *List.SortStrategy(Descending);*
Template Method	Defines the skeleton of an algorithm in an operation, deferring some steps to subclasses.	*Template A = new Student();* *Template B = new Teacher();* *A.Write(); B.Write();*
Visitor	Represents an operation to be performed on the elements of an object structure.	*List.Add(Student("A");* *List.Add(Student("B");* *List.Visit(new VoteVisitor());*

You don't need to memorize or fully understand all these patterns yet; instead, make a mental note of this list as a reference for the future. You'll see more about some of these patterns and how you can implement them concretely in the sample LOB application (CRM software) that you will create during the course of this book. You'll also see why you should choose a specific pattern for a specific problem. Of course, you won't use them all here, because some are solutions to problems that you will not encounter in a normal MVVM application. Still, it's worth having the list, and I suggest that you study and experiment with these patterns, because the only way to master all of these different approaches is to understand them in the context of experience.

As developers start to learn the GOF patterns, they typically try to apply the same pattern to every solution—but that approach is incorrect. For example, if you were building a Windows Service, it would probably be over-engineered if you were to apply the MVVM pattern to it.

UI Design Patterns

A full branch of design patterns is dedicated to building UIs. The best-known UI design patterns are the Model View Controller (MVC), the Model View Presenter (MVP), and the Presentation Model (PM) patterns that you encountered in the book's introduction as fore-bears of the MVVM. Other UI patterns exist as well. These are subpatterns of the MVC and MVP patterns, but they are rarely implemented any more with the .NET Framework.

The UI is probably the most volatile part of an application, because it's subject to frequent changes over time. Inexperienced developers tend to bind the UI and the Model together, putting business logic related to the Model into UI code, which leads to unmaintainable applications. Another common problem is that inexperienced developers tend to mix in the UI part of the presentation logic with some business logic and some UI logic. By doing this, the testable surface of your application becomes smaller and smaller, and it becomes difficult to test and maintain the application Separation of Concerns (SoC).

Before starting to talk about the available design patterns and into which types of technology they best fit, let me clarify when you should use a design pattern for the UI, and when you should not. The main purpose of these patterns is to separate the business logic from the UI, to make the UI more testable and maintainable, and to preclude the need to write business logic in the UI, which is something that you should always avoid.

Many developers misunderstand this fundamental concept and try to make the UI totally agnostic—they try to separate the Model from the UI completely. But that approach is wrong because the UI, usually defined as a View, has some dependencies on the Model; the View is designed to display the information provided by a specific Model or by a set of Models. This information is then manipulated by an intermediary object, which is the ViewModel in the MVVM pattern.

Creating a generic View is a pretty cool accomplishment, but it's not the purpose of a UI design pattern. However, the inverse of this is not true: it's important to keep the Model agnostic and unaware of the View because you might want to recycle the Model to use it with additional Views or in other applications. For now, remember that building an agnostic

View is *not a requirement* of a UI pattern. I'll also mention here that the Model will contain business logic related to the business operation that it can execute. In any case, this business logic should never include any presentation or UI logic, because as discussed earlier, the Model is View-independent.

You should also keep in mind that the UI patterns you'll analyze in the next sections are suggestions and guidelines to make the UI testable and maintainable—but they are not constraints. Especially with a flexible pattern like MVVM, you might need to design some hybrid solutions to satisfy specific problems that do not fit in the basic structure of the pattern.

A Little Taste of History

The father of all the UI design patterns is the MVC pattern, first described in 1979 by Trygve Reenskaug, a software developer working for Smalltalk at Xerox. In the original MVC pattern, the View was in charge of managing the graphical controls displayed on the screen, the Controller was in charge of interpreting the keyboard and mouse inputs, and the Model was the object in charge of managing the data and the behaviors of the application domain.

Over the years, MVC has split into two branches: passive MVC, where the Controller is in charge of controlling the View and the Model, and active MVC, where the View actively interacts with the Model and listens to its changes.

In the early 1990s, developers at Taligent Corporation began to adopt an alternative interpretation of the MVC, the MVP pattern, which removed the Controller and introduced the Presenter. This approach is significantly different because the Presenter is aware of the Views, and each View knows its Presenter. This pattern has been widely adopted in both web and client applications.

In 2004, Martin Fowler introduced his set of enterprise design patterns, which included the father of the MVVM pattern, the PM pattern. Unfortunately, due to its strict requirements, the PM pattern was never as successful as the MVC or the MVP patterns, largely because it was designed for a technology like Windows Presentation Foundation (WPF), which wasn't yet released.

In 2005, Microsoft applied the PM pattern to WPF, introducing a PM-derived pattern specifically tailored for WPF, the MVVM pattern, which fully exploits the binding engine power of WPF and Silverlight.

The MVC Pattern

The MVC pattern comprises three objects, each one in charge of a specific function in the UI context. You can apply the MVC pattern in a web application (which is a stateless application by design) where the Controller is in charge of processing user inputs and coordinating server-side calls until the View is rendered (as with ASP.NET MVC); however, you can also apply this pattern to a stateful Client UI technology such as Windows Forms or WPF.

In MVC:

- The Model represents the data in the application in a logical way; it is in charge of carrying the data and making other objects aware of data changes.

- The View is the graphical representation of the Model; it is responsible for displaying the Model data in suitable form.

- The Controller is the orchestrator of this pattern; it is in charge of intercepting user input (mouse and keyboard) and interacting with the Model and/or the View.

Figure 2-1 shows the structure of a basic MVC design. This design is also called the Passive MVC pattern, and it's the default implementation.

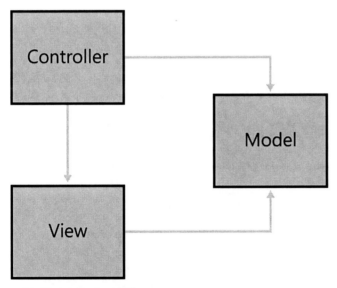

FIGURE 2-1 A Passive MVC pattern.

The most important point of this implementation is that the Model is aware of neither the View nor the Controller. The Model remains agnostic, so you can develop and test it in a separate context. However, the View and the Controller are both aware of the Model: the View because it's in charge of displaying the Model's data, and the Controller because it's the bridge between user input and the Model's changes. Finally, the View and the Controller are aware of each other; in the default passive implementation the Controller knows its Views, but Views are unaware of their Controller.

Listing 2-1 is a theoretical implementation of an MVC pattern in C#. This example uses the framework ASP.NET MVC.

LISTING 2-1 MVC pattern using ASP.NET MVC V2 and C#

```
/// <summary>
/// Simple Model that represents an Employee entity
/// </summary>
public class Employee
{
    /// <summary>
    /// The First Name
    /// </summary>
    public string FirstName { get; set; }

    /// <summary>
    /// The Last Name
    /// </summary>
    public string LastName { get; set; }
    /// <summary>
    /// The Company name
    /// </summary>
    public string Company { get; set; }
}


///<summary>
/// The Controller in charge of displaying the Views
///</summary>
public class HomeController : Controller
{
    /// <summary>
    /// An action that renders the Index View
    /// </summary>
    public ActionResult DisplayEmployee()
    {
        var model = new Employee
        {
            FirstName = "John",
            LastName = "Smith",
            Company = "Microsoft"
        };
        return View(model);
    }
}

<h2>DisplayEmployee</h2>
<fieldset>
        <legend>Fields</legend>
        <div class="display-label">FirstName</div>
        <div class="display-field"><%: Model.FirstName %></div>
        <div class="display-label">LastName</div>
        <div class="display-field"><%: Model.LastName %></div>
        <div class="display-label">Company</div>
        <div class="display-field"><%: Model.Company %></div>
</fieldset>
```

The implementation of the MVC pattern in Listing 2-1 uses a simple Model: an employee that represents a business object. The Controller is in charge of creating the Model based on a "new employee" request made by a user. When the user makes a new employee request, the Controller creates a new instance of a specific View and injects the Model into that View. Finally, the View renders the Model by using some HTML tags and the MVC Framework binding syntax.

Of course, in a real application you would have a service or a Data Layer that retrieves the Model from the database and sends it to the Controller. Figure 2-2 shows the process flow of this implementation.

Controller
Model
View
Request Employee
Service
Update
Get

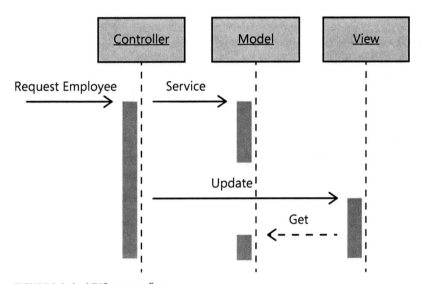

FIGURE 2-2 An MVC request flow.

Figure 2-3 shows the final result as it might appear in a browser.

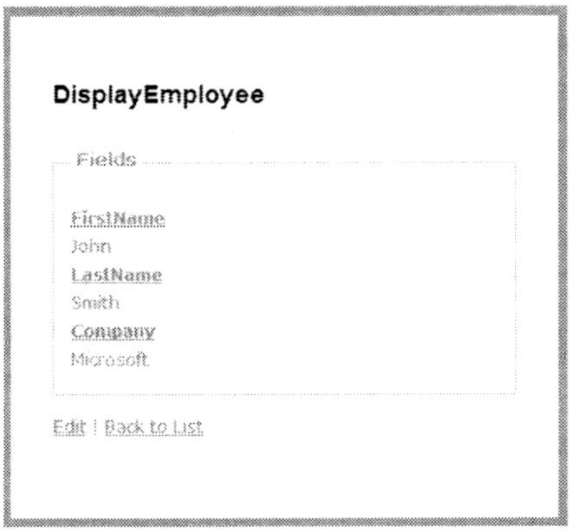

DisplayEmployee
Fields
FirstName
John
LastName
Smith
Company
Microsoft
Edit | Back to List

FIGURE 2-3 The final result of an MVC application using ASP.NET MVC.

Pros and Cons of the MVC Pattern

The MVC pattern fits web applications best. Its strengths are its capacity to display the same Model in different Views and the ability to change the way the View renders without affecting the Model (which is unaware of the Views). Another strength is its testability. Because the View is also unaware of the Model, the Controller can simply use a mockup Model for testing purposes. That makes MVC a good fit for a Test-Driven Development (TDD) approach.

That said, the MVC pattern can be also used in client applications that are not stateless (such as web applications). In fact, there are popular MVC frameworks specifically for client technologies such as Windows Form or Java.

On the other hand, MVC is a complex pattern, and it is event-driven; the Controller reacts to changes made by users, about which it notifies the Model and the View. In addition, updating MVC can can consume a considerable amount of resources, because the View must be alerted and updated through the Controller for every update. Some of the modern frameworks such as ASP.NET MVC do not apply the MVC pattern in its original form—another reason why this pattern a good fit for both client and web applications.

In addition, the *original* MVC pattern, as it was conceived, would not be a good fit for new UI technologies such as WPF and Silverlight. With that said. I would also like to specify that there are many modern UI design patterns today that are wrongly identified with the name "MVC pattern," but these are not the original MVC pattern; they're substitutes for the original pattern.

The MVP Pattern

The MVP pattern is categorized either as an evolution of the MVC pattern or a different interpretation of it. The main difference is that in the MVP pattern, the View and the Presenter are connected using a different approach. In MVC, the View is totally independent; in MVP the View is passive and delegates any action to the corresponding Presenter. Another important difference is that in MVP, the Presenter interacts with the View using a binding engine or a custom implementation of a binding engine if the UI technology doesn't provide one. The View and Model are not connected in MVP, while in MVC, the View is totally or partially aware of its corresponding Model.

Like the MVC, the MVP has three components, but with some differences:

- The Model is the same as in MVC. It represents any business entity with associated data and business logic.

- The View is the graphical interface in charge of rendering the data. It directly references the Presenter so that it can delegate to it the interpretation of all user interactions.

- The Presenter drives the UI logic; it knows both the View (through an interface) and the Model. It updates the View based on change notifications from the Model and updates the Model based on change notifications from the View. This is the object that encapsulates the presentation logic, and it usually sets property values and calls methods on the View rather than using a binding engine.

The MVP pattern has been implemented in both client and web applications. You might read that the MVP pattern fits best with web applications, but in my personal experience, because its design is so dependent upon the Presenter, it's a better fit for a client application, although it is flexible enough to be used for a web application. Figure 2-4 shows the passive implementation of the MVP pattern.

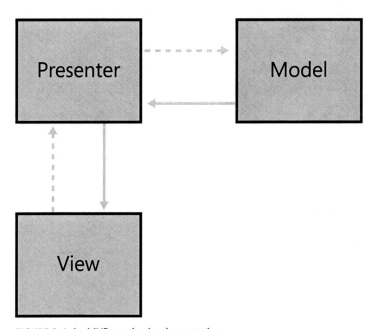

FIGURE 2-4 An MVP passive implementation.

Listing 2-2 shows a simple Windows Form example that illustrates how to implement the MVP passive view pattern in a simple client application.

LISTING 2-2 MVP implementation using Windows Form and C#

```csharp
/// <summary>
/// The Employee View contract
/// </summary>
public interface IEmployeeView
{
    /// <summary>
    /// The Firstname
    /// </summary>
    string FirstName { get; set; }

    /// <summary>
    /// The Lastname
    /// </summary>
    string LastName { get; set; }

    /// <summary>
    /// The Company name
    /// </summary>
    string Company { get; set; }
}

/// <summary>
/// The Employee presenter in charge of
/// driving the UI logic
/// </summary>
public sealed class EmployeePresenter
{
    /// <summary>
    /// The current view
    /// </summary>
    private IEmployeeView view;

    /// <summary>
    /// Initializes a new instance of the <see cref="EmployeePresenter"/> class.
    /// </summary>
    /// <param name="view">The view.</param>
    public EmployeePresenter(IEmployeeView view)
    {
        this.view = view;
    }

    /// <summary>
    /// Initializes this instance.
    /// </summary>
    public void Initialize()
    {
        var model = new Employee
        {
            FirstName = "John",
            LastName = "Smith",
            Company = "Microsoft"
        };
```

```
                //Bind the Model to the View
                UpdateViewFromModel(model);
        }

        /// <summary>
        /// Updates the view from model.
        /// </summary>
        /// <param name="model">The model.</param>
        private void UpdateViewFromModel(Employee model)
        {
            this.view.FirstName = model.FirstName;
            this.view.LastName = model.LastName;
            this.view.Company = model.Company;
        }
    }

    /// <summary>
    /// Concrete View.
    /// </summary>
    public partial class EmployeeView : Form, IEmployeeView
    {
        /// <summary>
        /// The corresponding presenter
        /// </summary>
        private EmployeePresenter presenter;

        /// <summary>
        /// Initializes a new instance of the <see cref="EmployeeView"/> class.
        /// </summary>
        public EmployeeView()
        {
            InitializeComponent();
            this.presenter = new EmployeePresenter(this);
            this.presenter.Initialize();
        }

        /// <summary>
        /// The Firstname
        /// </summary>
        /// <value></value>
        public string FirstName
        {
            get { return txtFirstname.Text; }
            set { txtFirstname.Text = value; }
        }
    /// omitted
    }
```

This example still uses the model *Employee* you saw in Listing 2-1. As you might have
noticed, the most significant difference from the MVC pattern is that the MVP View is totally
unaware of the Model it is rendering because the data is bound into the View controls by the

Presenter. Whereas the View is totally dependent on the Presenter, it must have a reference to it, because the View doesn't know how to react to user input. Figure 2-5 shows the final result.

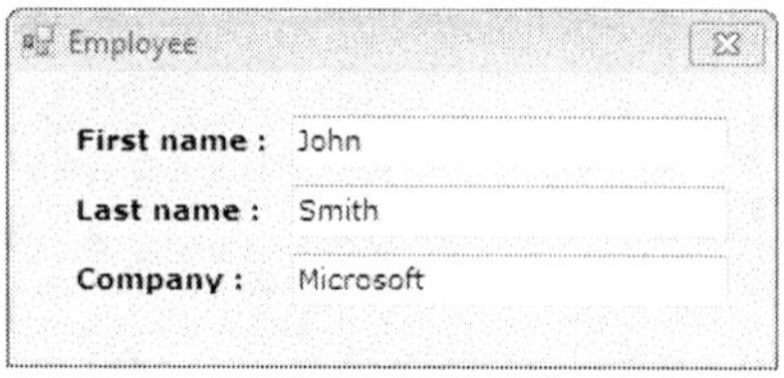

FIGURE 2-5 The MVP Passive View final result.

Pros and Cons of the MVP Pattern

What distinguishes the MVP pattern from other UI patterns are its roles and responsibilities. In the MVP pattern, the Presenter drives all logic; the View can only make notifications about user interactions to the Presenter, which can then call methods and change data on the View and/or on the Model.

Another problem lies in the round trip that occurs each time a user interacts with the View; the View must call a Presenter method, and then the Presenter must update the View.

MVP isn't appropriate for WPF or Silverlight because its passive implementation doesn't use the power of XAML's binding engine, and it's not able to cleanly separate the XAML code that constructs the UI from the procedural C# needed in the View for it to know its corresponding Presenter. I would discourage you from using the MVP pattern in WPF and Silverlight applications. If you are planning on using it, you might find that you don't need either of these technologies, and that classic Windows Forms technology might be better.

The big downside of MVP is that all presentation logic and every binding process must go through the Presenter, so if you plan to adopt a Supervising Presenter pattern (more on this in the next section) in WPF or in Silverlight, you will wind up with a View that has the Model as its DataContext, plus a separate reference to the Presenter.

Alternative Approaches to MVP

Another approach is the MVP *Supervising Presenter*. In this variant, the View is not passive; it knows the Model it is rendering, and requires a data binding engine to react to changes in the Model. The Presenter's role diminishes such that it's in charge only of intercepting user input that isn't to be handled by the Presenter. You might think that this approach would be interesting if applied to WPF or Silverlight—and it probably is when you need to work with a View/Model combination in which the interaction between them is very complex. On the other hand, the View has multiple references to maintain, which is difficult to test and requires more interfaces to maintain loose coupling. Finally, it's also complex because you must write code in the UI to manage the interaction with the Presenter. Figure 2-6 shows the MVP Supervising Controller structure.

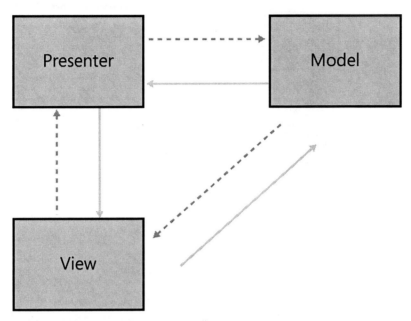

FIGURE 2-6 The MVP Supervising Controller.

The PM Pattern and MVVM

This section covers both the PM and the MVVM patterns because they are closely related to each other. The PM pattern appeared when technologies such as WPF and Silverlight were not yet available. When they did appear, Microsoft applied the PM pattern to WPF and Silverlight using the MVVM pattern.

The guiding principles of the PM are to maintain a loosely-coupled relationship between the PM and the View by making the View an observer of the PM, and using data binding to accomplish that. The PM knows the Model, but it doesn't specifically need to know the corresponding View. The View knows its PM only and exclusively through the binding engine. The power and flexibility of WPF/Silverlight data binding make this a suitable pattern for use in WPF/Silverlight applications.

The MVVM pattern is an evolution of the PM pattern that has the three usual principal components: a Model that represents the business entity (like the *Employee* class example), a View that is the XAML UI, and the PM or View Model, which contains all the UI logic and the reference to the Model, so it acts as the Model for the View.

Figure 2-7 contains a diagram that shows how to implement the MVVM pattern. Of course, this is a generic implementation. During the course of this book, you'll see that you need to implement the MVVM pattern in different ways depending on the type of View you are using, which can increase the complexity compared to that shown in Figure 2-7.

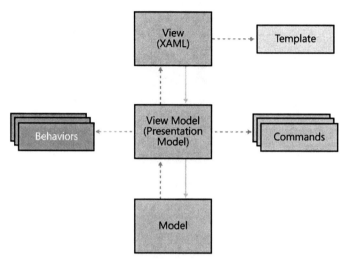

FIGURE 2-7 The basic structure of an MVVM application.

If you are planning to work with WPF or Silverlight, you must take advantage of the power-ful binding engine provided by these technologies. By doing this, your ViewModel should implement some specific interfaces required by the binding engine of WPF and Silverlight.

One of these is the *INotifyPropertyChanged* interface, introduced with .NET Framework ver-sion 2.0. This interface implements a notification system that activates when the value of a property changes. It's required in the ViewModel to make the binding engine of XAML work properly.

Another customization of the PM is the Command exposed by the interface *ICommand*, which is available for WPF and Silverlight. This specific Command can be bound to any XAML control and determines whether the control can or cannot execute a specific action. In WPF, this Command has a more powerful implementation through the Routed Command, which is a Command routed through the Visual Tree of a WPF UI.

A third customizable component is the *DataTemplate*, an XAML structure that defines how to render a specific ViewModel, or a specific state of the ViewModel. *DataTemplate* components are really views that are rendered at runtime by the WPF/Silverlight engine. They are particu-lar type of Views that cannot contain any code behind because they are dynamically created. Logically you are displaying a ViewModel or Model directly in the UI, but the view is conjured up at runtime and attached to the ViewModel or Model (through the data context).

Listing 2-3 shows a simplified example of implementing the MVVM pattern in WPF. In the next chapters, you'll see how you can customize every ViewModel component.

LISTING 2-3 MVVM implementation using WPF 4

```
/// <summary>
/// ViewModel for the Employee view
/// </summary>
public sealed class EmployeeViewModel : INotifyPropertyChanged
{
    public EmployeeViewModel()
    {
        var employee = new Employee
        {
            FirstName = "John",
            LastName = "Smith",
            Company = "Microsoft"
        };

        //Bind the model to the viewmodel
        this.Firstname = employee.FirstName;
        this.Lastname = employee.LastName;
        this.Company = employee.Company;
    }

    #region INotifyPropertyChanged
    /// <summary>
    /// Occurs when a property value changes.
    /// </summary>
    public event PropertyChangedEventHandler PropertyChanged;

    /// <summary>
    /// Called when [property changed].
    /// </summary>
    /// <param name="name">The name.</param>
    public void OnPropertyChanged(string name)
    {
        var handler = PropertyChanged;
        if (handler != null)
        {
            PropertyChanged(this, new PropertyChangedEventArgs(name));
        }
    }
    #endregion

    /// <summary>
    /// Private accessor for the Firstname
    /// </summary>
    private string firstname;

    /// <summary>
    /// Gets or sets the firstname.
    /// </summary>
    /// <value>The firstname.</value>
```

```
        public string Firstname {
            get
            {
                return firstname;
            }
            set
            {
                if (firstname != value)
                {
                    firstname = value;
                    OnPropertyChanged("Firstname");
                }
            }
        }
    }
// omitted
}
```

```xml
    <Window.DataContext>
        <vm:EmployeeViewModel />
    </Window.DataContext>
    <StackPanel Orientation="Vertical">
        <TextBlock>FirstName :</TextBlock>
        <TextBox
                Text="{Binding Path=Firstname,
                Mode=TwoWay,
                UpdateSourceTrigger=PropertyChanged}" />
        <TextBlock>Lastname :</TextBlock>
        <TextBox
                Text="{Binding Path=Lastname,
                Mode=TwoWay,
                UpdateSourceTrigger=PropertyChanged}" />
        <TextBlock>Company :</TextBlock>
        <TextBox
                Text="{Binding Path=Company,
                Mode=TwoWay,
                UpdateSourceTrigger=PropertyChanged}" />
    </StackPanel>
```

Again, this example uses the *Employee* concept from Listing 2-1. In it, you can see a simple ViewModel, which is nothing more than a class that implements the *INotifyPropertyChanged* interface and exposes the Model properties that you want to render in the UI. The View is an XAML window that uses the ViewModel instance as the data source, and that binds each property of the ViewModel to a specific control.

Because Microsoft Visual Studio 2010 has full support for the WPF and Silverlight binding engine, and because you are binding the *Employee* in the ViewModel constructor, you don't even need to run the application to view the final result—the View is functional even in design mode in the Visual Studio IDE, as illustrated in Figure 2-8.

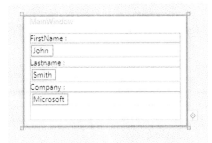

FIGURE 2-8 A functional MVVM application in the Visual Studio 2010 designer.

MVVM Pros and Cons

First, in the pro column, the MVVM pattern is designed for use with WPF or Silverlight, but it's not completely restricted to those technologies; you can implement MVVM in Windows Forms or with another UI technology as well. However, the power and flexibility of WPF or Silverlight (including features such as data binding, XAML, data templates, behaviors, and so on), make MVVM much easier to implement on WPF/Silverlight.

The ViewModel is the core of an MVVM application, so you must consider all the appropriate precautions, or you might easily end up with an unstable and messy application. Follow the guidelines carefully, and experiment with different solutions.

Don't try to fit your ViewModel into a strange architecture simply because you don't know how to write a specific behavior or *DataTemplate* in WPF or Silverlight. The pattern is designed for these technologies, so you should master them before mastering the MVVM pattern itself.

Finally, one key advantage of adopting the MVVM pattern is that the View is an observer of the ViewModel, which makes it easier to build the UI separately, and it lets you replace the View later or even at runtime, without the need to touch the presentation logic at all.

Advanced Design Patterns and Techniques

The design patterns available in the GOF patterns were created and adopted to solve some common problems related to object-oriented programming, such as how to create an object or how to open a dialog between two different objects. The UI patterns were designed and adopted to separate the business logic from the user interface, and to make the UI testable and flexible. As architecture advanced, these basic techniques were unable to satisfy larger architectural requirements. The solution gave rise to common solutions now called *enterprise patterns* or *patterns for enterprise applications*.

This book does not cover all the available enterprise patterns and techniques, but it will provide an overview of the common enterprise patterns and show in detail those that are fundamental to adopting MVVM.

> **More Information**   Read *Pattern of Enterprise Application Architecture* by Martin Fowler, and *Domain Driven Design* by Eric Evans, the founders of the Enterprise Architecture patterns. These two books are mandatory reading, in my opinion, for any senior developer or software architect, especially those who plan to build complex LOB MVVM applications.

Martin Fowler has exhaustively covered all of these patterns and divided them into in 10 different categories, each specific to a particular context. The first category is the *domain logic* pattern, which you'll analyze in the next chapter. There are three categories related to the Data Layer, which you'll cover in depth in Chapter 4, "The Data Access Layer." There are two patterns for concurrency and session state that are not used in this book. In the next section, you'll cover two particular patterns/approaches that are mandatory for an MVVM pattern or, in general, for any LOB application: the Dependency Injection pattern, also known as Inversion of Control, and the Domain Specific Language (DSL) pattern. You'll also get an introduction to the TDD approach, an agile technique for testing an application during its development phase.

The Inversion of Control Pattern

The term Inversion of Control (IoC) is a computer programming technique wherein the flow of the control of an application is inverted. Rather than a caller deciding how to use an object, in this technique the object called decides when and how to answer the caller, so the caller is not in charge of controlling the main flow of the application.

This approach makes your code flexible enough to be decoupled. It can be unaware of what is going on in the call stack because the called object doesn't need to make any assumptions about what the caller is doing.

The Dependency Injection pattern is simply a concrete implementation of the IoC. Unfortunately, as Martin Fowler specifies in his book, there is a lot of confusion about these terms, because the common IoC containers available for languages such as Java or .NET are typically *identified* as IoC containers, but the techniques *implemented* in your code when you use these frameworks is the Dependency Injection pattern, which is just one of the available concrete implementations for IoC. For example, if you plan to work with a modularized WPF/Silverlight application using a well-known framework such as Prism, you might implement IoC using the Service Locator pattern and not Dependency Injection because you need a global IoC container available for all the modules.

Imagine that you have a simple *LogWriter* concept that is used to write a log message either to a specific database table or to a specified file. You might depict this as shown in Figure 2-9.

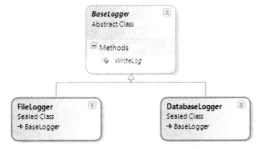

FIGURE 2-9 Basic structure of a multi-targeted log system.

The UML diagram in Figure 2-9 is pretty clear; there's an abstract *BaseLogger* class that exposes a *WriteLog* message, and two concrete classes that inherit from *BaseLogger*. These expose the method in two ways: one writes a log message to a database, the other to the file system. The following code shows the *wrong* way to use one of these concrete loggers—without applying an IoC implementation:

```
static void Main(string[] args)
{
    /* Wrong way
     *
     * */
    var firstLogger = new FileLogger();
    firstLogger.WriteLog("Some Text.");
    var secondLogger = new DatabaseLogger();
    secondLogger.WriteLog("Some other Text.");
    Console.ReadKey();
}
```

The biggest problem with this approach—not applying an IoC implementation—is that if you want to specify a different log at runtime, you'll need to rewrite some code. That's a huge architectural constraint. For example, suppose that you want to get rid of the *FileLogger* object. That's not easy. You can't simply eliminate it, because the application wouldn't execute any more, or at least, you would need to modify and recompile it for it to continue working.

To solve the problem, the first step is to decouple the existing hierarchy by using an interface instead of the base abstract class, as illustrated in Figure 2-10. This way, you simply define a contract between a concrete log and its interface. Subsequently, to write a log message to a different location, you just need to render the interface in a specific way.

FIGURE 2-10 Refactoring the *LogWriter* using a common interface.

The code that follows is a refactored version that uses an IoC approach to declare the type of logger to be used at runtime. This approach is still procedural, because it decides which logger to use, but at least it decouples the code, so this is a somewhat more flexible version of the custom writer.

```
/// <summary>
/// Custom writer that can uses any log
/// </summary>
public sealed class Writer
{
    /// <summary>
    /// Accessor to the injected logger
    /// </summary>
    private ILogger logger;

    /// <summary>
    /// Initializes a new instance of the <see cref="Writer"/> class.
    /// </summary>
    /// <param name="logger">The logger.</param>
    public Writer(ILogger logger)
    {
        this.logger = logger;
    }

    /// <summary>
    /// Writes the specified message.
    /// </summary>
    /// <param name="message">The message.</param>
    public void Write(string message)
    {
        this.logger.WriteLog(message);
    }
}
```

At this point, you need something between the application and the logger that can resolve which logger to use at runtime. The following example uses procedural code to do that without using the Dependency Injection or the Service Locator patterns:

```
static void Main(string[] args)
{
    // IoC without an IoC container
    var firstLogger = new FileLogger();
    //Injectin of a specific logger
    var writer = new Writer(firstLogger);
    writer.Write("Log for the File system.");
    Console.ReadKey();
}
```

An alternative solution would be to implement the Dependency Injection or the Service Locator. Figure 2-11 shows the main difference between these two different approaches.

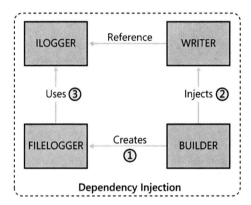

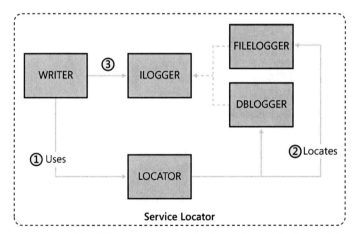

FIGURE 2-11 The differences between the Dependency Injection and the Service Locator patterns.

In the next section, you'll see how to implement these two techniques using Microsoft Unity or Microsoft Managed Extensibility Framework.

Microsoft Unity

Microsoft Unity is an application framework that is delivered as part of the Microsoft Enterprise library, but you can also download it as a standalone component from CodePlex at *http://unity.codeplex.com*. As of this writing, the latest version is 2.0, available for WPF and Silverlight. You can also use Microsoft Unity in any other type of .NET application.

Unity is an extensible Dependency Injection container through which you can apply Dependency Injection in your code using either a declarative approach (XML) or a procedural approach (C# or Visual Basic .NET). With Unity, you can inject code into constructors, properties, and methods.

Unity has an extensible core engine called "container" that implements the interface *IUnityContainer* (you can inherit from this if you need to extend the existing implementation). It has three principal methods which it uses to register an instance, retrieve a specific instance, and define the lifetime of an object. Figure 2-12 shows the basic structure of Unity.

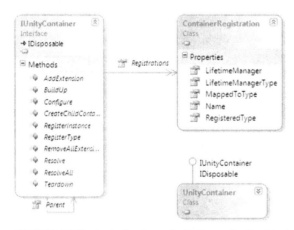

FIGURE 2-12 The basic structure of a Unity application block.

Dependency Injection with Unity

In this first example, you'll see how to define a policy for a specific logger and use it in your applications. In this case, the logger is declared in the container, and then the example assigns Unity the responsibility of creating the logger.

To implement this, change the code in the Writer constructor to specify that Unity will be in charge of creating this object at runtime using the *[InjectionConstructor]* attribute.

```
/// <summary>
/// Initializes a new instance of the <see cref="Writer"/> class.
/// </summary>
/// <param name="logger">The logger.</param>
[InjectionConstructor]
public Writer(ILogger logger)
{
    this.logger = logger;
}
```

Now you can change the code to register the type of logger that you want to use along with the type of writer, and leave the responsibility of creating the objects to Unity.

```
//Prepare the container
var container = new UnityContainer();
//We specify that the logger to be used is the FileLogger
container.RegisterType<ILogger, FileLogger>();
//and how to instantiate a new Writer
container.RegisterType<Writer>();
//Here Unity knows how to create the new constructor
var writer = container.Resolve<Writer>();
writer.Write("Some Text.");
```

Beyond that, you can use Unity to implement all aspects of the Dependency Injection pattern. For example, you can write some policies that define how long an instance of a specific object should stay alive, or you can intercept object creation and change the code injected at runtime using specific behaviors.

Service Locator with Unity

Another possible implementation of the IoC pattern is to use the Service Locator.

> **Note** You might read on the Internet that the Service Locator is an anti-pattern, because its decoupling is too high, and that you should not use it because it can prevent you from knowing if your code executes correctly outside the runtime context, thus making your code less testable. Or you might read that you totally lose control of the injection because the resulting code is more decoupled than when using Dependency Injection. I disagree, as the next example shows.

To see how you can write a Service Locator using Unity, there is nothing better than some sample code. To use the Service Locator with Unity you need an adapter, which you can find on the CodePlex website at *http://commonservicelocator.codeplex.com*. This adapter was built to apply the Service Locator pattern with any of the available IoC containers for .NET, including Unity, Castle, Spring, StructureMap, and so on.

First, you create a simple adapter (provider) so you can use the Microsoft Service Locator in conjunction with Unity, as shown in the following:

```
/// <summary>
/// Utility to configure the container
/// </summary>
public sealed class UnityContainerConfigurator
{
    /// <summary>
    /// Configures this instance.
    /// </summary>
    /// <returns></returns>
    public static IUnityContainer Configure()
    {
        var container = new UnityContainer()
        .RegisterType<ILogger, FileLogger>()
        .RegisterType<Writer>();
        return container;
    }
}
```

Then you implement the writer using the Service Locator instead of Unity (of course, you know that this is not totally true, because you're using the Unity container behind the scenes); what the developer will see here is a Service Locator implementation:

```
// create a new instance of Microsoft Unity container
var provider = new UnityServiceLocator(UnityContainerConfigurator.Configure());
// assign the container to the Service Locator provider
ServiceLocator.SetLocatorProvider(() => provider);
// resolve objects using the service locator
var writer = ServiceLocator.Current.GetInstance<Writer>();
writer.Write("Some Text.");
```

In this case, the created provider instantiates and registers a new Unity container. It then assigns the provider to the *ServiceLocator* instance, and finally, resolves the objects by using the Service Locator.

As you probably noticed, the primary difference is that with the Dependency Injection pattern, you control the creation and the flow of the code. In contrast, when using the Service Locator, you no longer control how or what to create; you simply call the common Service Locator and get an instance of the available component.

Typically, you'd use the Service Locator in decoupled applications for which the developer doesn't have access to common components that aren't referenced in the current assembly. The Service Locator covers that gap.

The Managed Extensibility Framework

Managed Extensibility Framework (MEF) is an application block introduced in .NET 3.5 as a beta experiment from Microsoft Labs and then implemented as part of the .NET 4 Framework. It is available for both WPF (common CLR) and Silverlight.

MEF is not really an IoC container, or more accurately, it is not *only* an IoC container, it's a framework to manage extensions and plug-ins. Choosing to use MEF doesn't mean that you can't use Unity for the basic IoC operations; the two are parallel and different application blocks. In addition, Unity is more powerful for Dependency Injection, because that's its main target, while the main target of MEF is application composition.

Like Unity, MEF has a catalog and a container that are in charge of discovering and rendering an instance of a registered object at runtime. But more than that, with MEF you can declare some specific components on a separate assembly and register them in the MEF catalog. You can then access the catalog from the client application at runtime and use these components. The main difference is that MEF is not a Dependency Injection container; it's an extensible framework to resolve additional components at runtime. Its main priority is to make large applications extensible. Figure 2-13 shows the basic structure of MEF.

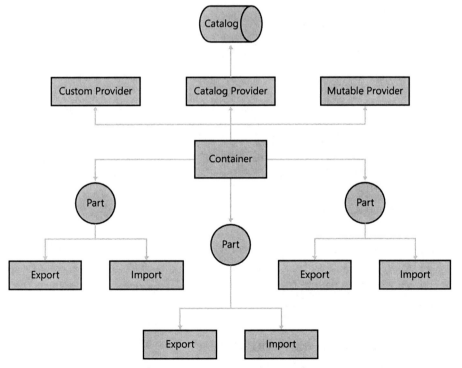

FIGURE 2-13 The composition of the MEF Framework (source: MSDN library).

To use MEF, you need to write a custom logger that satisfies the MEF design requirements. In this case, you want to specify how MEF should export and use the logger.

```
/// <summary>
/// Logger customized for MEF
/// </summary>
[Export(typeof(ILogger))]
public class MefLogger : ILogger
{
    /// <summary>
    /// Writes the log.
    /// </summary>
    /// <param name="message">The message.</param>
    public void WriteLog(string message)
    {
        Console.WriteLine("String built from MEF: {0}.", message);
    }
}
```

At this point, you can use the program and declare an MEF property. Next, you need to instantiate the MEF catalog; here, the code declares that the catalog is the executing assembly. Then you can easily use the components.

```
/// <summary>
/// Gets or sets the writer.
/// </summary>
/// <value>The writer.</value>
[Import]
public ILogger Writer { get; set; }

public void Run()
{
    // first we build the catalog
    var catalog = new AssemblyCatalog(Assembly.GetExecutingAssemb
    //create the container using the catalog
    var container = new CompositionContainer(catalog);
    container.ComposeParts(this);
    //use the resolved property
    Writer.WriteLog("Mef message");
}
```

The approach here is significantly different than using an IoC container. With MEF, you prepare a catalog of components and then access them directly. Notice that this example does not in any way control how to create a new instance of a logger, it simply starts the MEF engine.

Differences Between MEF and Unity

To wrap up this discussion, I want to focus your attention on what an IoC container is, what an extensibility framework like MEF is, and why you should use one instead of the other.

The main reasons to use Unity (or any other IoC container) are if:

- You have dependencies between your objects.

- You need to manage the lifetime of an object.

- You want to manage dependencies at runtime, such as cache, constructors, and properties.

- You need to intercept the creation of an object.

The main reasons to use MEF are if:

- You need to implement external and reusable extensions in your client application, but you might have different implementations in different hosts.

- You need to auto-discover the available extensions at runtime.

- You need a more powerful and extensible framework than a normal Dependency Injection framework, and you want to get rid of the various boot-strapper and initializer objects.

- You need to implement extensibility and/or modularity in your components.

If your application doesn't require any of the items in these lists, you probably should not implement the IoC pattern, and you might not need to use Unity and MEF.

DSLs: Writing Fluent Code

The Fluent Interface approach we are going to view now is not specifically related to the MVVM pattern, and it doesn't need to be implemented in order to obtain good results with the MVVM pattern.

On the other hand, as this approach is used in this book when I talk about MVVM and how to write some custom factories used to build the ViewModels, I believe it is worthwhile to spend some time taking a look at it, if only to see what it is and how it works.

The domain-specific language (DSL) approach instigates another interesting discussion about enterprise patterns. DSL is a technique to make code fluent and readable for a specific context. For example, when you write a query for Microsoft SQL Server, you work with a DSL language known as T-SQL; it's a domain-specific language because it doesn't work outside the specific context of writing queries for SQL Server. The main purpose of this technique is to make the code more readable inside the context where it's supposed to be used, helping to reduce mistakes and misunderstanding.

You might need to implement a custom DSL language in your application to avoid mistakes or improper implementations by other colleagues. For example, you might have a small MVVM framework that needs to be implemented in a specific order, and you would like to avoid changes in the call stack order. When a DSL is built for an internal use, it takes the name *fluent interface*, which is a term that was first coined by Martin Fowler and Eric Evans when they were writing about Enterprise patterns.

The following code shows how you might write a fluent interface by using C#:

```
Var mvvmView = FluentEngine
   .BuildCommands()
   .BuildData()
   .InitView()
   .Create();
```

You could write the same thing using a normal approach in this way:

```
Var mvvmView = new MvvmView();
mvvmView.BuildCommands();
mvvmView.BuildData();
mvvmView.InitView();
```

You might agree with me that you can read the first implementation with greater ease. A second important point though, is that the first implementation provides a constraint. Using the fluent approach, a developer cannot initialize the View before calling the initialization of the Commands and the Data.

This approach can be very easy to implement, but it must be designed carefully; otherwise, the DSL might end up using a custom dictionary that's not always readable and understandable for other developers, such as the code that follows:

```
Var mvvmView = FluentEngine
   .BuildPart01()
   .BuildPart02()
   .DoThis()
   .DoThat();
```

Of course, this is an extreme view of what a DSL implementation should look like, but it's better to get the team members to agree to the terminology so that you don't end up writing a DSL language that only you can understand.

Writing a Fluent Interface in C#

Microsoft's LINQ syntax is a good example of a fluent interface. The essence of LINQ is the *IQueryable* collection, whose methods always return another *IQueryable* collection. That makes it easy to "chain" the methods, so you can easily write code such as the following:

```
Var employees = employees
    .Where(x => x.FirstName == "John")
    .Where(x => x.Age > 35)
    .OrderBy(x => x.LastName)
    .First();
```

This fluent code will be translated by LINQ to SQL in something like the following:

```
SELECT TOP 1 FROM EMPLOYEE
WHERE FIRSTNAME = 'JOHN'
AND AGE > 35
ORDER BY LASTNAME
```

Consider for a moment how you create an object. Usually, you call the object constructor, often a parameterless constructor, and then assign a value to each property, such as this:

```
Var employee = new Employee();
employee.Firstname = "John";
employee.Lastname = "Smith";
employee.Age = 35;
```

This is pretty simple, but what if you want to know, in advance of creating the object, that the object will be valid, or ensure that *Employee.Age* will never be lower than 30? Unfortunately, you can't; instead, you need to remember to run some checks before using the created object.

However, if you were to refactor this code using the Factory pattern and a fluent interface, you could provide such constraints. To do that, you first need an interface to define the contracts available in the DSL object, such as the following:

```
public interface IFluentEmployee
{
    /// <summary>
    /// The Firstname.
    /// </summary>
    /// <param name="firstName">The first name.</param>
    IFluentEmployee FirstName(string firstName);

    /// <summary>
    /// The Lastname.
    /// </summary>
    /// <param name="lastName">The last name.</param>
    IFluentEmployee LastName(string lastName);

    /// <summary>
    /// The company name.
    /// </summary>
    /// <param name="company">The company.</param>
    IFluentEmployee Company(string company);

    /// <summary>
    /// Creates this instance.
    /// </summary>
    /// <returns></returns>
    Employee Create();
}
```

Now you can implement this interface in a custom class and massage the static methods, to make the code more fluent, as follows:

```csharp
/// <summary>
/// The Fluent creator
/// </summary>
public class FluentEmployee : IFluentEmployee
{
    private static Employee employee;

    private static IFluentEmployee fluent;

    /// <summary>
    /// Initializes a new instance of the <see cref="FluentEmployee"/> class.
    /// </summary>
    public FluentEmployee()
    {
        fluent = new FluentEmployee();
    }

    /// <summary>
    /// Inits this instance.
    /// </summary>
    public static IFluentEmployee Init()
    {
        employee = new Employee();
        return fluent;
    }

    /// <summary>
    /// The Firstname.
    /// </summary>
    /// <param name="firstName">The first name.</param>
    public IFluentEmployee FirstName(string firstName)
    {
        employee.FirstName = firstName;
        return fluent;
    }

    /// <summary>
    /// The Lastname.
    /// </summary>
    /// <param name="lastName">The last name.</param>
    public IFluentEmployee LastName(string lastName)
    {
        employee.LastName = lastName;
        return fluent;
    }

    /// <summary>
    /// The company name.
    /// </summary>
    /// <param name="company">The company.</param>
```

```
public IFluentEmployee Company(string company)
{
    employee.Company = company;
    return fluent;
}

/// <summary>
/// Creates this instance.
/// </summary>
/// <returns></returns>
public Employee Create()
{
    return employee;
}
}
```

Now, you can write a fluent interpretation of the *Employee* constructor in the following way:

```
var employee = FluentEmployee
    .Init()
    .FirstName("John")
    .LastName("Smith")
    .Company("Microsoft")
    .Create();
```

This is a simple task with far-reaching implications; it helps to ensure that any developer who uses the code won't misunderstand the methods. For example, it's pretty clear that the *FirstName()* method will change the value of the *Employee* instance's *FirstName* property.

You can now move forward and refactor this code again to define a specific order for this method or implement lambda expressions to make your DSL language totally dynamic.

You'll see a custom implementation of the DSL syntax in the Chapter 4 and subsequent chapters. For example, in Chapter 3, "The Domain Model," you'll see how to build a custom Factory and a custom Validator using the DSL technique and lambda expressions.

Introduction to TDD

TDD is a parallel programming technique of developing software by writing tests for it—even before you write the code. This is a topic that you'll revisit throughout this book; this section provides a brief overview of what TDD is.

With the MVVM pattern, you can use TDD, which works very well due to the decoupled nature of the MVVM pattern; TDD is not mandatory to use the MVVM pattern, but it is a very highly-suggested step.

That dovetails nicely with the main concept of TDD, which is to write the test for your code before writing the code itself. Any input you provide at this point would cause the test to fail.

Only then do you implement the code that would pass the test. Finally, you refactor the code and run the test to be sure that the refactor process has been implemented correctly.

At first, the idea of writing a test before writing the required code might sound strange, but you'll find that when you apply this pair-programming technique, you will write better code. In contrast, if you develop the code first, and then try to test it, it's far more difficult to guarantee that the code is implemented properly.

The motto of TDD is "red, green, refactor," which means, write the specifications, verify the code against those specifications, and then refactor.

A TDD Example

Here's an example that illustrates how you might write code using TDD. For consistency, this example also sticks with the by now well-known *Employee* entity. Simply right-click the *[TestMethod()]* text, and then select Add New Unit Test; the final result should appears as in the following example:

```
/// <summary>
///A test for Company
///</summary>
[TestMethod()]
public void CompanyTest()
{
    Employee target = new Employee();
    string expected = "Microsoft";
    string actual;
    target.Company = expected;
    actual = target.Company;
    Assert.AreEqual(expected, actual);
}
```

The preceding code verifies that the property *Company* in the class *Employee* is populated correctly. Of course, this is a simple (and probably inconclusive) test but it should serve to give you an overview of how TDD works.

Tools for Unit Testing

There are several good tools for building unit tests. In the interest of space, I'll limit the discussion to only two common ones. This book uses MSTest, which is the unit test tool that is delivered with Microsoft Visual Studio 2010 and Team Foundation Server (TFS). It is available through the Visual Studio IDE. Figure 2-14 shows the integration between Visual Studio and MSTest.

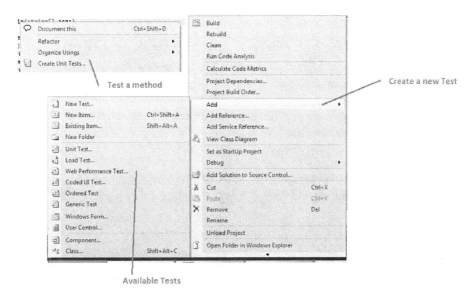

FIGURE 2-14 Available options for Visual Studio and MSTest.

If you're planning to use MSTest, you'll welcome its full integration into Visual Studio and TFS, which makes it easy to deliver your code with integrated tests during the build process. Another agile programming technique called Continuous Integration (CI) requires you to deliver a build of your code every day; to do that, the only possible safe approach is to implement TDD throughout your application and integrate it in into your build process. If you use Visual Studio 2010 with TFS, all these features are available in one environment.

Another famous test framework for .NET is NUnit, a ported version of the JUnit framework used in the Java language derived from xUnit. NUnit is written in C# and is fully .NET compliant.

NUnit is more flexible than MSTest, and it ships with both a command line and an integrated environment for Visual Studio. If you're planning to work using the TDD approach, you should give it a try. Unfortunately, syntax differs considerably between the various testing frameworks, so it's best to try all the available frameworks in advance, and then adopt only one.

Available Resources for TDD

TDD is a complex technique that can't be learned and implemented in a couple of days. To make it work, you need to implement it correctly. More important, TDD requires discipline and consistency.

For more reading about TDD, I recommend these books:

- *Test-Driven Development in Microsoft .NET*, by James W. Newkirk and Alexei A. Vorontsov (Microsoft Press, 2009; ISBN: 978-0-7356-1948-7)

- *The Art of Unit Testing*, by Roy Osherove (Manning, 2009; ISBN: 978-1-933988-27-6)

You can also find a useful list of TDD resources on the MSDN website at *http://msdn.microsoft.com/en-us/library/aa730844(VS.80).aspx*, or at this TDD development community site: *http://www.testdriven.com*.

In this book, you will often find references to TDD techniques, along with explanations of how to properly test the MVVM pattern implementations that are discussed here.

Summary

A design pattern is a guideline that identifies a common solution for a common problem but that might be adapted to the specific problem to which it is applied. The common design patterns are known as Gang of Four design patterns and classified into three categories: creational, structural, and behavioral. The classification is based on the type of problem the design pattern tries to solve.

An additional category of design patterns is composed of those used for user interfaces; in this category there are four major patterns: the MVC, the MVP, the PM, and the MVVM. While the MVC and the MVP are more generic and flexible, the MVVM is specifically designed for WPF and Silverlight.

Yet another category of design patterns is known as Design Patterns for the Enterprise, or Architectural Design Patterns. Martin Fowler and Eric Evans classified these patterns, and you'll find them explained in the book *Patterns of Enterprise Application Architecture*. The IoC pattern is just one of these Enterprise Patterns. It's useful for moving the dependencies inside a called object from a caller object.

Testing your application is fundamental to avoiding bugs and runtime errors. If you implement TDD techniques from the outset, you can guarantee that your application is following the design requirements and that your code has been tested before moving the application to a production environment.

Chapter 3
The Domain Model

After completing this chapter, you will be able to:

- Understand Domain-Driven Design techniques.
- Create a validation mechanism for the Domain Model.
- Create a sample Domain Model.

Introduction to Domain-Driven Design

The key role of software is to solve problems and fulfill requirements. Of course, this can be accomplished in different ways. One way is by using Domain-Driven Design (DDD). With DDD, you try to solve the business problems that characterize the Domain Model by creating a set of Domain Entities that represent the various business parts of the application.

Using the DDD technique, you write an application that has a firm foundation, based on an object-oriented approach. You develop the code around the business entities that compose the business domain and then adapt it to satisfy the business relationships between the entities and their behaviors.

DDD is a set of methodologies and technologies applied to a specific context, so implementation can be very different from one application to another. The main objective of a DDD application is to focus on understanding and modeling the Domain (the business requirement), which is possible only when the development team already has a deep knowledge of the business requirements. For this and other reasons, DDD can usually be achieved only when the team works in parallel with a group of analysts who already know the business requirements of the application. If you and your team decide to apply the DDD technique, you are essentially agreeing to define a common language focused on the Domain Model designed for the application, which will reduce the language gap between analysts, architects, and developers. In fact, when you start to develop an application that involves people from different backgrounds (such as the aforementioned analysts, architects, or developers) you will find that each will typically define the same thing using different terminology. The DDD technique should be able to bridge this gap.

Because the DDD approach acts as a communications channel between the project members, it is essential that the language defined for the Domain Model is unambiguous and clear. If the Domain Model is well defined and the domain language is clear and reflects the domain behaviors and relationships, the business logic of the entire domain will be clear and understandable, as well—to all the members of the project, whether they are analysts, architects, or developers. The language you create using the Domain Model should let you identify gaps and mistakes in the model, because it is the only bridge between you and the model.

One fundamental requirement of DDD is to isolate the Domain from the rest of the application; you need to keep the Domain Model as a pure language construct for your domain problem. With that said, it's pretty clear that the DDD approach requires a lot of additional effort, and you should probably consider it only when the domain problems are relatively complex and the application is relatively large. By that, I mean that you probably shouldn't consider the DDD as a feasible approach for a very simple application because of its high cost. Still, I personally always use the DDD approach, even for very small domains composed of only two or three domain entities. I believe that the DDD approach gives my applications a very high level of flexibility for future growth.

As a summary of this brief introduction to the DDD approach, here are the main benefits of applying the DDD technique to your application:

- **Common Language**   If you define a common domain for your application you will create a common language usable in the same way and with the same meanings by all the team members.

- **Extensibility**   The DDD approach lets you create an extensible application because the domain is the core of the application—and by design a domain is extensible and loosely coupled, so it should be relatively easy to extend and implement new features in an existing domain model.

- **Testability**   A DDD application is testable by design.

DDD Terminology

To understand and model a domain, you need an introduction to the common terminology used in this set of techniques so that you can understand how DDD is structured.

- The *Domain* is the set of activities, knowledge, and contexts with which the application is developed; it is specific to the business context of the application.

- The *Model* is part of the Domain. It usually represents a specific set of aspects related to the Domain, and is composed of a set of entities and value objects.

- An *entity* is a unique object represented in the Domain by a Domain Entity. Domain Entities are unique and do not change when the application state changes. An entity encapsulates properties, behaviors, and states. For example, the *Customer* object of the sample CRM application is a Domain Entity.

- A *value object* is an object used to describe some aspect of the Domain but that is immutable and doesn't have a unique identity in the Domain. For example, a *Customer* might have a list of *Addresses*; one of these *Addresses* is a value object because it is used to describe an address of a Domain Entity of type *Customer*.

- *Aggregate roots* are root entities used to control relationships between child entities or child value objects. They typically control access to these child objects and/or to control the interactions between them.

- The *ubiquitous language* is language constructed around the Domain that developers and analysts will use to specify a particular aspect of the Domain.

- The *context* is clearly the world in which the model can exist.

Analyzing the CRM Domain

With those definitions in place, you can start with the "user stories" that represent the CRM application example.

 Note A user story captures a requirement, task, or part of a business process that the user will carry out when using the application. It describes the business process in an understandable way for both users and developers.

The design of this application will be domain-driven (a concept analyzed in depth in this chapter), so the domain is the first component that needs to be designed. This domain-first design is the typical approach you will use when developing MVVM applications using DDD for the Domain Layer.

The user story is the draft of the business space; it describes how the various elements of the domain interact and how specific tasks or business processes will be accomplished. There are usually several user stories for an application, not just one.

The sample CRM application that you'll build in this book is composed of some user stories which are summarized in the following paragraph as a set of macro user stories:

> *"As an Employee, I want to be able to add and manage Customers."*
>
> *"As an Employee, I also want to be able to manage Orders submitted by a Customer."*
>
> *"As an Employee, I also want to verify that a specific Product ordered by a Customer is available in stock."*
>
> *"As a Customer, I want to Order any available Product."*

That's pretty simple. It's a pity that this clear and complete statement doesn't really offer much guidance to developers. So first, you need to extract the core concepts of this user story.

The statement indicates one domain that we will call CRM.Domain, and four principal entities: an *Employee*, a *Customer*, an *Order*, and a *Product*. You will need to add additional components to these major models, such as an *Address*, a *Contact*, an *OrderLine*, and so on.

Using a piece of paper and a pencil to create a rough model, we end up with something like Figure 3-1. This is the first draft of the Domain Model. As you proceed through this chapter, you will see how to evolve and compose each part of this domain and use it in an MVVM application.

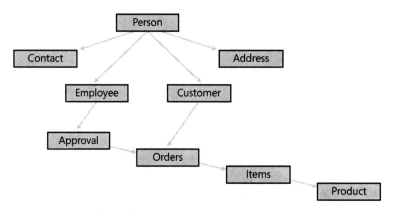

FIGURE 3-1 A mockup of the CRM Domain Model.

You can compare this diagram to a set of simple objects modeled in C# or Visual Basic .NET, where each shape represents nothing more than one or more classes with relationships that can be properties, complex objects, a collection of child objects, or a reference to a parent object.

Domain Entity and Data Transfer Object

Let's start with the definition of a Domain Entity and a Data Transfer Object (DTO), with the understanding that you'll keep these concepts in mind for the remainder of the book. I've used the following convention syntax in this book; you might find different definitions, but the concepts that I expose here are the basic concepts of DDD and not a merely a personal interpretation.

A Domain Entity, also known as a Domain Object, is a component of the Domain Model that represents the uniqueness of an element in the business domain, and that maintains the state of that element. For example, in the CRM Domain Model, the *Employee* entity is a Domain Entity.

A DTO is a flat object—it's serializable, and used to transfer data between layers, objects, and/or tiers. It doesn't have any business logic, and usually, it doesn't have any circular references to parent or child objects. Software architects such as Martin Fowler use the term *Value Object* to define a simple object in the Domain Model that doesn't have a specific identity.

The concept of a DTO is mandatory in DDD, and here's why. Imagine that the MVVM application has a simple XAML combo box that you want to populate with all the available employees in the database. You might easily come up with something like this:

```
// C# code to retrieve the data
Var employees = dataLayer.GetAllEmployees(); // this returns an IList<Employee>
// Pseudo XAML
<combobox
    ItemSource="{Binding Path=employees}"
    DisplayMemberPath="FirstName"
    SelectedValuePath="Id" />
```

In the preceding code, a big problem is that you are truly binding the entire employee entity. Even though the code uses only the first name and the ID, in reality, you're holding the entire object in memory. For example, if the *Employee* has a list of *Address* entities mapped as a property, the code also carries that list along in memory.

The solution is to flatten this object by using a DTO that will represent only the data needed at the moment. An entity might have one or many DTOs, depending on the context. The following example uses a LINQ extension to create a new list of DTOs, starting from a list of entities.

```
Public class EmployeeDto
{
    string FirstName { get; set; }
    Guid Id { get; set; }
}

// C# code to retrieve the data
Var employees = dataLayer
                .GetAllEmployees()
                .Aggregate(new List<EmployeeDto>() => (list, obj)
                {
                    var dto = new EmployeeDto { FirstName = obj.FirstName, Id = obj.Id };
                    list.Add(dto);
                    return list;
                });
// Pseudo XAML
<combobox
    ItemSource="{Binding Path=employees}"
    DisplayMemberPath="FirstName"
    SelectedValuePath="Id" />
```

There are two more considerations about entities and DTOs. First, note that although business logic was not discussed, it should be included in the Domain Entities and in the Domain

Services. You'll see why in future chapters. The second consideration lies in the way you can map an entity against a DTO, and vice versa. You'll see how to use reflection or emit to create a simple auto-mapper component for your applications, and how to use existing tools such as Auto-Mapper (*http://automapper.codeplex.com*) or Emit Mapper (*http://emitmapper.codeplex.com*).

Here's a brief summary of what a Domain Entity is, along with its common characteristics and constraints:

- A Domain Entity should be implemented using persistence ignorance; it should not be aware of how it is persisted in a database or when it should be persisted. You want to be able to use the domain across multiple applications and across multiple storage types.

- A Domain Entity represents a specific problem of the domain, but it is not a business object; it encapsulates only the business logic required, and nothing more. If you want to add business logic to a Domain Entity, you should consider building a specific Business Object (this is discussed in future chapters).

- A Domain Entity should be aware of its validation and its constraints as related to other Domain Entities available in the same Domain. It should use a clear naming convention, and it should reflect the ubiquitous language using only the native properties and methods of the entities.

The POCO Object and the O/RM

In the previous section, you saw that the unique role of a Domain Entity is to address a specific area or aspect in the domain. This concept is clear, but it's a far cry from the reality of a real-world application. Based on DDD definitions and paradigms, a Domain Entity should be a POCO object, or rather, an object that doesn't know anything about its persistence, and that doesn't inherit specific classes before it can be persisted or used with a specific framework.

Referring back to the previous example, you might have noticed that I added an *ID* property to the *Employee* entity to specify its uniqueness in the collection, such as in a database table. Without the ID, you would not be able to identify the selected *Employee* in the *ComboBox*. In DDD, the Domain Entity should be a POCO (.NET) or POJO (Java) object. In my opinion, this concept works only in the abstract; it is not feasible in practice.

I also want to expound upon the importance of identity for a Domain Entity. Suppose you have two *Employee* entities, defined as follows:

```
Var employee = new Employee { FirstName = "John", LastName = "Smith", Age = 54 }
Var employee = new Employee { FirstName = "John", LastName = "Smith", Age = 23 }
```

Without attaching some sort of *UniqueId* to each one, you wouldn't be able to distinguish between them. This isn't an unrealistic example; it's highly likely that an organization might have two different employees with the same *FirstName* and *LastName*, but who have different ages or different roles in the system.

To work with an O/RM such as the Entity Framework or NHibernate (as you will in this book or in any other multi-tiered application), it will be mandatory, by design, to add a constraint to such entities that makes them unique in the model. Therefore, you must give them an identity—just as you would with the rows of a table, using the primary key. This requirement does not mean that the entities are not POCO, but it does break the perfect design of a POCO object.

Another question revolves around *persistence ignorance*, which occurs when your classes and the surrounding application layers don't know or care how their data is stored. For example, in the .NET 3.5 version of Entity Framework, if you wanted to use pre-existing classes, you had to modify them by forcing them to derive from *EntityObject*. In .NET 4, this is no longer necessary. You don't need to modify your entities for them to participate fully in Entity Framework operations. This allows you to build applications that embrace loose coupling and Separation of Concerns. With these coding patterns, your classes are concerned only with their own jobs. Many layers of your application, including the UI, have no dependencies on external logic, such as the Entity Framework APIs, yet those external APIs are still able to interact with your entities.

In conclusion, the concept of POCO (POJO) objects is neat and clear in DDD, but unrealistic in a real-world application. As I have mentioned before, remember that the concepts are guidelines, not policies, so you should follow them when possible, and then adapt your code to meet your specific needs.

Development Approaches of a Domain

Martin Fowler's book, *Patterns of Enterprise Architecture Application* (PoEAA), mentions three different approaches for developing the Domain.

Taking the concept of a Domain as just a general definition, Fowler says that you can develop an application using one of the three available patterns for the Domain: the Transaction script, the Active Record, and the Domain Model.

The DDD approach described in this book uses the Domain Model approach, but for simpler applications, you might consider using the Active Record approach, or if you just need to write a sequential set of commands, you would probably want to use the Transaction Script approach. It's worth exploring why and when you should use each of these patterns.

Transaction Script

The Transaction Script approach is often used by non-expert developers in situations such as a junior developer's first project or for a simple utility script. The main concept of the Transaction Script is to organize all logic primarily as a single procedure, making calls directly to the database or through a thin database wrapper. Each transaction will have its own Transaction script, although common subtasks can be broken into subprocedures.

For example, you might need to write a function that will print out a list of available employees. To do that using the Transaction Script approach, you would write code similar to that shown below, where the connection, the SQL statements, and the C# code are mixed together in a single step.

```
Var connection = new SqlConnection();
var command = new SqlCommand(connection, "SELECT * FROM EMPLOYEE");
var reader = command.ExecuteReader();
Connection.Open();
while(reader.Read())
{
    Console.WriteLine("Employee: {0} - {1}" reader["FirstName"], reader["LastName"]);
}
// end of pseudo code …
```

You might agree with me that this piece of code is faster to develop and easier to read and change than a layered application approach, but it's absolutely unmaintainable and redundant. That's because if you later decide that you need to execute that same query within some other function, you would have to copy (or rewrite) the same code—and every time you need to change something you would have to make that change in every piece of code that uses that SQL statement. In addition, this code is non-testable, because the database logic and the code are totally bound together without any architectural logic.

Using the Transaction Script approach becomes untenable when the single transaction code (procedure) becomes complex. Eventually, you will want to break the code into a smaller set of transactions that are called sequentially by a main task. That's the point where you begin to completely lose control of your application. Every time you have a bug, the only solution is to debug the full stack.

I simply don't recommend this technique for any situation—except when you have sequential steps that need to be executed and the flow of these sequential steps will never change during the evolution of the software, such as in the following pseudo code:

```
Public void ApproveOrder()
{
    VerifyOrder(order);
    VerifyCustomer(customer);
    AssignOrder(employee, order);
    ApproveOrder(order);
}
```

In this case, the workflow sequence is a requirement of the Domain Entity Order before an order can be approved. Most probably, this workflow will never change, so you can use the Transaction Script approach in this type of situation successfully. Still, note that this example is just a sequence of methods; it doesn't embed SQL calls or UI calls within a single method.

Database-Driven Approach

Often, developers don't have the power to design an application from the beginning, for many different reasons. For example, you might be tasked with rewriting an existing legacy system where the database can't be altered, and it's difficult to design a domain that fits the existing database. Or you might have scarce programming resources, and the lifetime of the application will be short, such as a utility that will run for few months. These cases aren't conducive to writing a complex tiered system that will possibly take more time to develop than the expected application lifetime.

The database-driven approach forces you to adopt the Active Record pattern. In this pattern, the main player of the application is the database, and you design the domain to reflect the structure of that database. Therefore, you will have a Domain Entity for each table in the database and the needs of the database drive the application flow.

This approach is not wrong—especially if you have just started to use the DDD approach but haven't yet mastered it. Many O/RMs, such as Entity Framework or NHibernate, offer the possibility of creating an Active Record domain without losing the power of a relational model and a Data Layer; unfortunately, this approach is still far away from the more robust and complex DDD approach.

In this case, because the object (entity) is a specular image of the relative database table, the object itself must be in charge of updating its status against the database, and must also be aware of how it's saved and retrieved from the database, so you'd typically see code such as:

```
Var employee = New Employee().Get(1);
employee.FirstName = "John";
employee.Save();
```

I would say that if you need to write a simple data-entry application that doesn't include any complex business logic or any data transactions, the Active Record pattern is probably a good starting point. Remember however, that it would be both the starting and ending point; this pattern can't be extended or changed like DDD. Another problem with this pattern is that because entities have full control of the persistence process, a developer can easily write code that will incorrectly drop or change an existing record.

In my opinion, you should avoid this pattern when designing complex and extendable Line of Business (LOB) applications, because:

- Versioning of a record with the Active Record patterns is a nonsensical approach. The "active" entity is the row in the database, so if you want to keep a history of data changes, you have to clone the active record whenever it changes, storing the older version and replacing it with the new version.

- You cannot separate state and behavior, because the entity is in charge of persisting itself and also holds its data structure. In other words, with Active Record, entity state and behavior are wrongly mixed together, such as in the *Save()* command or the *IsNew* property.

- There's no Separation of Concerns, and the code is difficult to test. For one thing, the entity works only if the database is available, so you can't test the entity by itself without also testing the database—and that breaks one of the principles of Test-Driven Development (TDD), because the tests cannot be as independent as they should be.

Domain-Driven Approach

The Domain-Driven approach is the concrete implementation of the DDD technique. In this case, you have a Domain that drives the entire application. The Domain is totally unaware of any corresponding database. To make everything simpler, you can use an O/RM, such as Entity Framework or NHibernate, to help create the correct SQL code to persist the entities in the database.

DDD is the most complicated approach because it requires more time, more tests, and more agility, and because it also requires a deep knowledge of the business processes. In the end, though, it is also the most flexible and maintainable approach because the Domain and the database are not closely related. Suppose that next month, your company has decided to switch from SQL Server to MySQL. By using the DDD approach, you will only need to change the connection string in your O/RM. Or suppose that the order approval process changes, because of some restrictive policies introduced in the accounting department. With DDD, you will just need to identify that process in the model and update it.

With the Domain-Driven approach, you usually work with an O/RM and have a *UnitOfWork*, which is a component that keeps the database session alive so that you can execute create, read, update, and delete (CRUD) operations against it. You'll analyze this pattern in detail in the next chapter, when you build the Data Layer for the sample CRM application. With the *UnitOfWork* and the DDD, you would execute the code you saw in the Transaction Script section this way instead:

```
Var employees = unitOfWork.Get<Employee>();
foreach (var employee in employees)
{
    Console.WriteLine("Employee: {0} {1}", employee.FirstName, employee.LastName);
}
```

You saw in the chapter introduction why you should use the Domain-Driven approach and why it's more flexible than other approaches. As you go forward, just keep in mind the highlights listed here:

- DDD is business oriented, so you don't need to know all the available tables in a database to commit a business transaction with your code; the Domain "speaks for itself" and it's self-explanatory, providing ubiquitous language

- The Domain is extensible and recyclable because the only constraint is the business around it and nothing else, such as a database or framework

- Your application becomes plug-and-play because the Domain (the business core) isn't constrained to a specific technology. If you need it for another application, you can just add it as a component and use it

- It's totally testable; you can test the Domain before you have any database or UI ready for testing. You can also expand or evolve and retest it repeatedly during your application's evolution.

How To Create an Object In DDD

In object-oriented programming (OOP) syntax, you usually create non-static objects using the *new* keyword. The process is similar but a little bit different in C#, Visual Basic .NET, or Java. When you need a new instance of an object, you simply create it using the *new* keyword, and then start using it, for example, by changing some property values or calling a specific method.

Using the constructor method, you can come up with two different choices; you can create a parameterless constructor or a constrained constructor that will force developers to provide specific values when creating the object.

```
//parameterless
var employee = new Employee();
employee.FirstName = "John";
employee.LastName = "Smith";
employee.Age = 54;

//constructor with parameters
var employee = new Employee("John". "Smith", 54);
```

Both methods work fine. The first one is probably more "open" because it doesn't force developers to specify anything—they can simply create an empty new *Employee* object. The second one is more data driven because it requires a specific *FirstName*, *LastName*, and *Age* to work. (You can also use C# 4 optional parameters to avoid the last one, but in that case you can set up default values that might be incorrect for that Entity type.)

When you start to work with MVVM, the first problem you will encounter from an architectural point of view is that the application is layered, so the developer who wrote the Domain Model might not be the same as the developer(s) who will use it in the ViewModel or Business Layer. For these reasons, you must apply some constraints on how to create a new Domain Entity to ensure that the entity is valid and created correctly.

The factory pattern, discussed in Chapter 2, "Design Patterns," is an object-creational pattern designed to drive the creation of a specific object. The factory pattern is mandatory in a DDD application because it drives developers to create entities using specific guidelines and it supports TDD. The following example illustrates why:

```
//factory for Employee
var employee = Factory.CreateEmployee("John", "Smith", 54);

// throw exception because the age can't be lower than 1
var employee = Factory.CreateEmployee("John", "Smith", 0);

//here we have some business logic that we may not need to know
var employee = Factory.CloneEmployee(anotherEmployee);
```

The preceding code forces developers to create a new *Employee* through the available factory methods; if the developer enters an invalid age, for example, the factory will simply throw an exception. The same is true for the cloning process; using the factory method forces the developer to clone an employee in a predefined way, driven by the Domain logic.

Factory Patterns

If you plan to use the factory method in your Domain you will guarantee a constraint in the creation of a new Domain Entity in the entire project. Factory patterns are divided into two subpatterns: the abstract factory and the factory method. The main difference between these two creational patterns is that the first one defines a generic factory that's in charge of creating any object, as shown in the following code:

```
Var employee = AbstractFactory.CreateEmployee();
var order = AbstractFactory.CreateOrder();
```

In contrast, the Factory pattern is oriented more toward the Domain Entity, so you will have a factory class for each available entity in the domain:

```
Var employee = EmployeeFactory.Create();
var order = OrderFactory.Create();
```

Which method you use is up to you, but you should consider the maintenance process when making a decision. For example, if you choose to use the abstract factory, whenever you need to change the creational process for a specific type, you might break the code for creating some other type. For simplicity, I use a custom implementation of an abstract factory/method.

The small Domain below (Figure 3-2) represents an *Employee* entity with a set of addresses. The first rule of the factory is that you can't create an *Address* without having it attached to a parent *Employee*, because an *Address* without an *Employee* doesn't have any logical business meaning in the Domain.

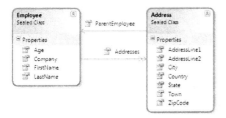

FIGURE 3-2 A sample Domain Model for the Factory Pattern.

The factory method/abstract factory implementation I use is represented by the following class diagram (Figure 3-3), which contains an abstract factory that defines the constraints in my code but has a concrete implementation of the factory for each Domain Entity, to provide more control and decoupling from the Abstract Factory pattern:

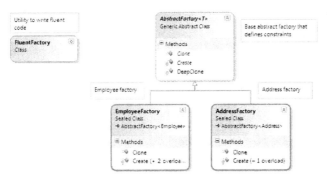

FIGURE 3-3 Implementation of the Abstract Factory pattern in conjunction with the factory method.

This architecture provides a clean way to create a new object for use in an application. For example, to create a new *Address*, you must specify a parent *Employee* entity, and to create a new *Employee*, you must provide the basic information required for an *Employee*:

```
// Create a new Employee
var employee = FluentFactory
    .Employee()
    .Create("John", "Smith", "Microsoft", 54);

// Create a new Address
var address = FluentFactory
    .Address()
    .Create(employee, "Main Street 14", country: "USA");
employee.Addresses.Add(address);
```

```
    // verify the object created
    Console.WriteLine("Employee: {0} {1} has {2} addresses.",
        employee.FirstName,
        employee.LastName,
        employee.Addresses.Count);
    Console.ReadLine();

    //clone the employee and change the first name
    var cloned = FluentFactory.Employee().Clone(employee);
    cloned.FirstName = "Sarah";

    // verify the cloned object
    Console.WriteLine("Employee cloned: {0} {1} has {2} addresses.",
        cloned.FirstName,
        cloned.LastName,
        cloned.Addresses.Count);
    Console.ReadLine();
```

You can still put constraints in your factory, such as throwing an exception if the value provided for a parameter is not correct (for example, the *Age* < 21) or if a value is not within a specified range, but at this point, you can make developers aware of the potential exceptions using Visual Studio decorations. Look at the following code used to create a new *Employee*:

```
/// <summary>
/// Creates the specified Employee.
/// </summary>
/// <param name="firstName">The first name.</param>
/// <param name="lastName">The last name.</param>
/// <param name="company">The company.</param>
/// <param name="age">The age.
/// </param>
/// <returns></returns>
/// <exception cref="System.ArgumentNullException">Thrown when the
/// Age is lower than 21</exception>
public Employee Create(
    string firstName,
    string lastName,
    string company,
    int age)
{
    if (age < 21)
    {
        /// <exception cref="System.ArgumentNullException">Thrown when
        /// the Age is lower than 21</exception>
        throw new ArgumentNullException("The Age should be greater than 21.");
    }
}
```

You might also consider leaving the factory wide open, and then implementing the validation pattern over the Domain Entity. You'll see more about the Validation Pattern in the next section.

Domain Entities Validation

Earlier, when discussing the Domain Model, I wrote that a Domain Entity should be agnostic against any framework or Data Layer: it should be a POCO object. For the same reason, a Domain Entity should not be aware of its validation, because that might differ between two different applications using the same Domain. Note that this is just my point of view; there are ongoing debates in the software architect community on where to place validation logic. Some believe it should be placed inside a Domain Entity while others believe it should be placed outside.

Validation is the process by which you verify that the data of a specific object or class is valid. To make that decision, you need a set of *validation rules* for each property that describes why and when the data might or might not be valid.

One possible way to provide validation support in the Domain Model is to provide a *layer supertype* (a common class or component used to incorporate common behaviors or properties used by all the classes or objects of that layer through inheritance from this supertype) that can delegate the validation of a specific entity to a separate validation service. This is what happens with the Entity Framework auto-generated model, in which each class inherits from a common base class that also provides validation support. An alternative method is to provide a parallel interface for validating a specific Domain Entity, using that Interface to keep the Entity itself unaware about the validation process.

Classic Validation

The example that follows shows the classic way of validating an object using a simple Validation Service, not generic, with embedded validation rules. First, there's a base class that defines the contract for the validator:

```
public abstract class BaseValidator<T>
{
    /// <summary>
    /// Determines whether the specified entity is valid.
    /// </summary>
    /// <param name="entity">The entity.</param>
    /// <returns>
    ///     <c>true</c> if the specified entity is valid; otherwise, <c>false</c>.
    /// </returns>
    public abstract bool IsValid(T entity);

    /// <summary>
    /// Gets or sets the errors.
    /// </summary>
    /// <value>The errors.</value>
    protected IList<ValidationResult> Errors { get; set; }
}
```

Next, you need to create a validator for each Domain Entity that you want to validate. Of course, using this approach, you can easily extend the validator for other objects, such as a ViewModel in a WPF/Silverlight application or a DTO for an RIA Service.

```csharp
public sealed class EmployeeValidator : BaseValidator<Employee>
{
    /// <summary>
    /// Determines whether the specified entity is valid.
    /// </summary>
    /// <param name="entity">The entity.</param>
    /// <returns>
    ///     <c>true</c> if the specified entity is valid; otherwise, <c>false</c>.
    /// </returns>
    public override bool IsValid(Employee entity)
    {
        var result = true;
        this.Errors = new List<ValidationResult>();
        if (entity.FirstName.Length < 10)
        {
            this.Errors.Add(new ValidationResult(
              "The Firstname should be greater than 10."));
            result = false;
        }
        if (entity.LastName.Length < 10)
        {
            this.Errors.Add(new ValidationResult(
                "The Lastname should be greater than 10."));
            result = false;
        }
        return result;
    }

}
```

You can easily test this code by verifying that the Domain Entity is not valid if you insert an empty *FirstName*, such as in the following:

```csharp
/// <summary>
///A test for IsValid
///</summary>
[TestMethod()]
public void IsValidTest()
{
    EmployeeValidator target = new EmployeeValidator();
    Employee entity = new Employee { FirstName = "", LastName = ""};
    bool expected = false;
    bool actual;
    actual = target.IsValid(entity);
    Assert.AreEqual(expected, actual,
      "The Entity should not be valid at this point.");
}
```

The main disadvantages of this approach are:

- It embeds the validation rules in a custom class that is difficult to document.

- The validation rules are composed of a set of *if* statements in procedural C# code; as the rule set becomes more complex, it becomes more difficult to test its correctness.

The advantage of using this approach is that the Domain Model is totally unaware of the available validation rules. You can use this Domain Entity with or without validation support, and you can change the validation depending on the context.

Validation Using Attributes and Data Annotations

In the .NET Framework 4, a namespace called *System.ComponentModel.DataAnnotations* is available for both the common CLR (WPF) and the lighter Silverlight CLR. You can use the *DataAnnotations* namespace for various purposes. One of these is for data validation using attributes, and another is the visual description of fields, properties, and methods, or to customize the data type of a specific property. These three categories are classified in the .NET Framework as *Validation Attributes*, *Display Attributes*, and *Data Modeling Attributes*. This section uses Validation Attributes to define validation rules for objects. You'll use the Display Attributes category in Chapter 6, "The UI Layer with MVVM," which is dedicated to the MVVM toolkit, and the Data Modeling Attributes in Chapter 4, "The Data Access Layer."

To use the *DataAnnotations* namespace, you need to add a reference to the assembly—that reference is not included in any Visual Studio project template by default. Then you need to decorate your objects with the correct attributes.

As an example, the code below uses an *incorrect* approach of decorating a Domain Entity directly with these attributes. Next, I will refactor this code to make that entity unaware of its validation.

```
public sealed class Customer
{
    /// <summary>
    /// Gets or sets the first name.
    /// </summary>
    /// <value>The first name.</value>
    [Required(ErrorMessage = "The FirstName is a mandatory Field")]
    [StringLength(10, ErrorMessage =
        "The FirstName should be greater than 10 characters.")]
    public string FirstName { get; set; }

    /// <summary>
    /// Gets or sets the last name.
    /// </summary>
    /// <value>The last name.</value>
```

```
[Required(ErrorMessage = "The LastName is a mandatory Field")]
[StringLength(10, ErrorMessage =
    "The LastName should be greater than 10 characters.")]
public string LastName { get; set; }

/// <summary>
/// Gets or sets the title.
/// </summary>
/// <value>The title.</value>
[Required(ErrorMessage = "The Title is a mandatory Field")]
public string Title { get; set; }
}
```

The *Customer* entity can be easily validated using a generic validator because you know that we want to validate only those properties that have a *DataAnnotations* attribute on them.

```
public sealed class GenericValidator<T>
{
    /// <summary>
    /// Validates the specified entity.
    /// </summary>
    /// <param name="entity">The entity.</param>
    /// <returns></returns>
    public IList<ValidationResult> Validate(T entity)
    {
        var results = new List<ValidationResult>();
        var context = new ValidationContext(entity, null, null);
        Validator.TryValidateObject(entity, context, results);
        return results;
    }
}
```

At this point, we can easily test the validator against the *Customer* entity, as follows:

```
/// <summary>
/// Determines whether this instance [can validate customer].
/// </summary>
[TestMethod]
public void CanValidateCustomer()
{
    Customer entity = new Customer { FirstName = "", LastName = "" };
    GenericValidator<Customer> target = new GenericValidator<Customer>();
    bool expected = false;
    bool actual;
    actual = target.Validate(entity).Count == 0;
    Assert.AreEqual(expected, actual,
        "The Entity should not be valid at this point.");

}
```

Now, to remove the validation from the Domain Entity you need to create an interface that represents the Domain Entity and that includes the validation rules, and then inherit the Domain Entity from this interface. At the end of this process, you should be able to write code like this:

```
/// <summary>
/// Determines whether this instance [can validate customer].
/// </summary>
[TestMethod]
public void CanValidateCustomer()
{
    Customer entity = new Customer { FirstName = "", LastName = "" };
    GenericValidator<ICustomer> target = new GenericValidator<ICustomer>();
    bool expected = false;
    bool actual;
    actual = target.Validate(entity).Count == 0;
    Assert.AreEqual(expected, actual,
      "The Entity should not be valid at this point.");

}
```

Available Validation Frameworks

The validation technique that was just presented is only one of the techniques available for .NET. The advantage of using *DataAnnotations* is that it plugs into WPF and Silverlight perfectly, and it is designed in a way that works throughout all the layers of an MVVM application. In the ViewModel section, you'll see why the *DataAnnotations* approach is the perfect match for WPF or Silverlight.

Another interesting framework created by Microsoft is the *Validation Application Block*, which is available with Microsoft Enterprise Library 5.0 (*http://entlib.codeplex.com/*). The Validation Application Block uses the same general approach—validating an object against a set of rules defined using attributes (data annotations) or an external XML file. The major difference from the *DataAnnotations* is the process you use to validate an object, but you should obtain the same final result.

Another framework, part of the open-source project NHibernate, is the *NHibernate Validation Framework*. This is available at *http://sourceforge.net/projects/nhcontrib/* as part of the NHibernate Contrib project. The main disadvantage of using this framework is that unless you are planning to use NHibernate as your O/RM, you will introduce an additional dependency in your layers that might not be needed. This framework also requires you to sully your entities with validation rules related to a specific O/RM.

To sum up, it's important to keep the Domain clean and unaware of the validation rules or methods you're using, but it's also important that you decide to use the appropriate framework for the type of application that you're writing. In this book, you'll largely use the data annotations feature provided in the .NET Framework.

Unit Test the Domain Model

You should create the process for testing the Domain Model before starting to write the code for the Domain Model itself; this will guarantee that you will test the code against the expected results rather than vice versa.

When you write a Domain Model, you usually include some small business rules in your code that should be validated so that you can be sure that the Model is working properly. For example, the CRM Domain Model will have a *Person* entity that will have a set of *Address* entities included in an *IList<T>* collection. We want to guarantee throughout the entire model context that a *Person* can have one, and only one, *Address* as the default address. Another rule is that unless specified, the first address added to a *Person* entity's *Address* list will be the default address.

For this example, you should be able to write a first test like this:

```
Var person = PersonFactory.Create();
var address01 = AddressFactory.Create();
var address02 = AddressFactory.Create();
person.AddAddress(address01);
person.AddAddress(address02);
Assert.IsNotNull(person.DefaultAddress);
Assert.IsTrue(person.DefaultAddress == address01);
```

Another test—boring but useful—is to test each property value of your entity before starting to validate the entity itself. For example, we might want to be sure that when we call the *FullName* read-only property of a *Person* entity, the result will be the *FirstName*, a space, and the *LastName*.

```
Var person = PersonFactory.Create("John", "Smith");
Assert.AreEqual(person,FullName, "John Smith");
```

Constantly testing the definition of your Domain Model against the rules of your Model is your blueprint for guaranteeing that any change to the Model won't adversely affect the existing data structure and the existing flow of the Model.

Validation is also another interesting part that must be tested to be sure that the approach is working as expected. The only problem you might have when testing validation is that you should hard code the validation rules in your tests to be sure that you are testing the correctness of the validation rule set; on the other hand, that's useful for tracking what you have changed in the validation rule set itself.

```
Var person = PersonFactory.Create("John", "Smith");
// Validate return a Boolean result
Assert.IsTrue(Validator.Validate(person));
var invalidPerson = PersonFactory.Create();
Assert.IsFalse(Validator.Validate(invalidPerson));
```

Sample Code: The CRM Domain Model

Beginning with this chapter, the end of every chapter contains a section called "Sample Code," which is where you'll build the CRM application using the knowledge acquired in the earlier parts of the chapter. In this chapter, you've seen what a Domain Model is, how it should be implemented and tested, and looked at factory implementation and the validation process.

So first, let's revisit the user story that was given to us from the customer when he called to get a new CRM application.

> *"As a Company that sells products, I want to be able to manage my Orders; I need a system that monitors the availability of the Products, a registry section to administer my Customers, and an approval process managed by one of the available employees registered in the system."*

I have identified this user story with one Domain composed of the entities in charge of administering employees, customers, and their information, and an entity in charge of making and approving an order, based on a list of submitted and available products.

The Person Context

An *Employee* and a *Customer* can be grouped by some common information, such as *FirstName*, *LastName*, and so on. But there are also properties that relate more to a *Customer* than to an *Employee*. For example, you might not care about displaying an address for an employee, but you might need to know how to contact him; on the other hand, the user probably needs to know everything about a customer who placed an order, because you must know where to ship the order and how to contact the customer if there is a problem with the submitted order.

Your Domain will have, for now, a very simple layer supertype that will be the *DomainObject* class. This class has only one property, *PrimaryKey*, of type *GUID*, which will help distinguish the various entities available in the Domain context. In the next chapter you'll see why it's important to decide the primary key type of an entity before deciding on the final data store.

 Note As a design choice I will decorate the Domain Entities with Validation Rules. I am doing this solely because I want to show how to use validation attributes—and at the same time you'll be able to explore the structure of the Domain Entities. For real-world applications, I suggest that you embed validation attributes on an external interface that will be implemented by the Domain Entity.

The following code shows the base *DomainObject* layer supertype:

```
/// <summary>
/// The basic Domain Object
/// </summary>
public abstract class DomainObject
{
    /// <summary>
    /// Gets or sets the primary key.
    /// </summary>
    /// <value>The primary key.</value>
    [Required(ErrorMessage = "The Primary Key can't be null or empty.")]
    public Guid PrimaryKey { get; set; }
}
```

The Model will contain another abstract class called *Person*, which defines some common properties and methods available for both *Employee* and *Customer* entities. The class must be abstract because we don't want this class used directly by some developer in the code by mistake, but at the same time, we don't want to write the same code twice.

```
public interface class Person : DomainObject
{
    /// <summary>
    /// Gets or sets the first name.
    /// </summary>
    /// <value>The first name.</value>
    [Required(ErrorMessage = "The FirstName can't be null or empty.")]
    public string FirstName { get; set; }

    /// <summary>
    /// Gets or sets the last name.
    /// </summary>
    /// <value>The last name.</value>
    [Required(ErrorMessage = "The LastName can't be null or empty.")]
    public string LastName { get; set; }

    /// <summary>
    /// Gets the full name.
    /// </summary>
    /// <value>The full name.</value>
    public string FullName
    {
        get { return String.Format("{0} {1}", FirstName, LastName); }
    }

    /// <summary>
    /// Gets or sets the title.
    /// </summary>
    /// <value>The title.</value>
    [Required(ErrorMessage = "The Title can't be null or empty.")]
    public string Title { get; set; }
```

```csharp
/// <summary>
/// Gets or sets the birth date.
/// </summary>
/// <value>The birth date.</value>
[Required(ErrorMessage = "The Birth Date can't be null or empty.")]
public DateTime BirthDate { get; set; }


/// <summary>
/// Gets or sets a value indicating whether this instance is active.
/// </summary>
/// <value><c>true</c> if this instance is active; otherwise, <c>false</c>.</value>
public bool IsActive { get; set; }



/// <summary>
/// Gets or sets the contacts.
/// </summary>
/// <value>The contacts.</value>
public IList<Contact> Contacts { get; set; }



/// <summary>
/// Gets the default contact.
/// </summary>
/// <value>The default contact.</value>
public Contact DefaultContact
{
    get
    {
        if (Contacts == null)
        {
            return null;
        }
        return Contacts.Where(x => x.IsDefault).FirstOrDefault();
    }
}


/// <summary>
/// Adds the contact.
/// </summary>
/// <param name="contact">The contact.</param>
public void AddContact(Contact contact)
{
    if (Contacts == null)
    {
        Contacts = new List<Contact>();
    }

    // If there are no default address, set this one as default
    if (Contacts.Where(x => x.IsDefault).Count() < 1)
    {
        contact.IsDefault = true;
    }
```

```
        //If this is the new default address
        if (contact.IsDefault)
        {
            foreach (Contact cont in Contacts)
            {
                cont.IsDefault = false;
            }
        }

        // If the address is not already in the list
        if (!Contacts.Any(x => x.PrimaryKey == contact.PrimaryKey))
        {
            Contacts.Add(contact);
        }
    }
}
```

You might already notice that this entity introduces two new entities: *Contact* and *Address*. The *Contact* entity will be exposed by both *Employee* and *Customer* entities, because we might need to have a default contact for each of them. The *Address* entity is exposed only by the *Customer*, because it is not part of the LOB application that we are building to make us aware of any specific address for an *Employee*.

```
public sealed class Contact : DomainObject
{
    /// <summary>
    /// Gets or sets the type of the contact.
    /// </summary>
    /// <value>The type of the contact.</value>
    public ContactType ContactType { get; set; }

    /// <summary>
    /// Gets or sets the name.
    /// </summary>
    /// <value>The name.</value>
    [Required(ErrorMessage = "The Name is a mandatory field")]
    public string Name { get; set; }

    /// <summary>
    /// Gets or sets the description.
    /// </summary>
    /// <value>The description.</value>
    [Required(ErrorMessage = "The Description is a mandatory field")]
    public string Description { get; set; }

    /// <summary>
    /// Gets or sets the number.
    /// </summary>
    /// <value>The number.</value>
    [Required(ErrorMessage = "The Number is a mandatory field")]
    public string Number { get; set; }
```

```
        /// <summary>
        /// Gets or sets a value indicating whether this instance is default.
        /// </summary>
        /// <value>
        ///     <c>true</c> if this instance is default; otherwise, <c>false</c>.
        /// </value>
        public bool IsDefault { get; set; }
    }
```

Note that the *Contact* entity introduces the first Enum in this application. Using Enums in a Domain is important because they're self-explanatory and totally eliminate mistakes that can occur when using plain strings or integer values.

The following *Address* entity is no different than the *Contact* entity except for the exposed properties.

> **Note** If you follow the Martin Fowler approach, you would classify the *Contact* and *Address* entities as Value Objects more than Domain Entities because they represent a small component of a bigger Domain Entity, but they are not really Domain Entities—they don't have an identity representation in the Domain.

```
    public sealed class Address : DomainObject
    {
        /// <summary>
        /// Gets or sets the address line1.
        /// </summary>
        /// <value>The address line1.</value>
        [Required(ErrorMessage = "The AddressLine1 is a mandatory field")]
        public string AddressLine1 { get; set; }

        /// <summary>
        /// Gets or sets the address line2.
        /// </summary>
        /// <value>The address line2.</value>
        public string AddressLine2 { get; set; }

        /// <summary>
        /// Gets or sets the town.
        /// </summary>
        /// <value>The town.</value>
        public string Town { get; set; }

        /// <summary>
        /// Gets or sets the city.
        /// </summary>
        /// <value>The city.</value>
        public string City { get; set; }
```

```
        /// <summary>
        /// Gets or sets the state.
        /// </summary>
        /// <value>The state.</value>
        [Required(ErrorMessage = "The AddressLine1 is a mandatory field")]
        public string State { get; set; }

        /// <summary>
        /// Gets or sets the country.
        /// </summary>
        /// <value>The country.</value>
        [Required(ErrorMessage = "The AddressLine1 is a mandatory field")]
        public string Country { get; set; }

        /// <summary>
        /// Gets or sets the zip code.
        /// </summary>
        /// <value>The zip code.</value>
        [Required(ErrorMessage = "The AddressLine1 is a mandatory field")]
        public string ZipCode { get; set; }

        /// <summary>
        /// Gets or sets a value indicating whether this instance is default.
        /// </summary>
        /// <value>
        ///     <c>true</c> if this instance is default; otherwise, <c>false</c>.
        /// </value>
        public bool IsDefault { get; set; }
    }
```

The Domain Entity *Employee* has been omitted because, as you can see from Figure 3-4, the implementation is self-explanatory; it inherits from the class *Person* and it doesn't have any additional properties.

In conclusion, we now have the two main entities of this Model: *Employee* and *Person*. The difference between them is, as pointed out previously, the *Addresses* list, but also, a *Customer* has a list of Orders while the *Employee* has a list of Approval.

Figure 3-4 shows the final diagram for the *Person* Domain. To save space, I haven't included the rest of the code here, but the full code is available with the downloadable companion content to this book (see the download instructions in the Introduction to this book).

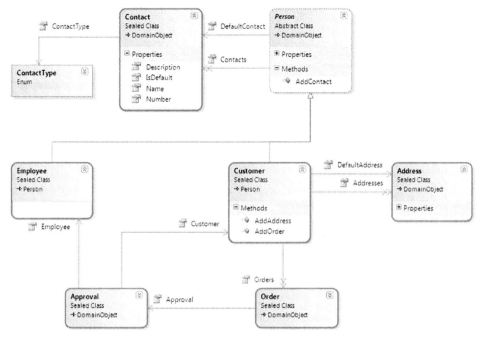

FIGURE 3-4 Part of the full Domain Model, the *Person* Domain.

The Order Domain

The CRM application example is in charge of monitoring the order process for a specific Customer/Products combination. The order process is composed of three major entities: the order itself, the order's list of items, and each item which is composed of a product, a quantity, a unit price, and a total amount based on an applied discount.

Going in reverse, the first entity we encounter is the *Product* entity, which represents a unique product in the company's stock. The *Product* is the Domain Entity in charge of representing a product and its properties throughout the entire domain. Figure 3-5 represents the full domain for an order process.

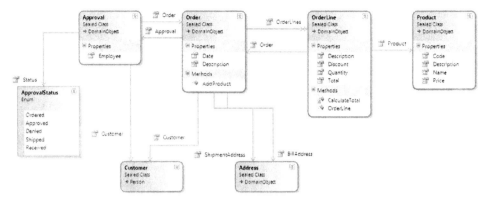

FIGURE 3-5 The Order Domain Model.

In the diagram, you can see the *Order* entity, exposed by an *OrderLine*, which identifies the amount and the total price for that *Order*. The *Order* has two *Address* references: one for the *BillingAddress* and one for the *ShipmentAddress*. Each *Order* is subject to an approval process that involves the *Order* itself, an *Employee*, and a *Customer*.

A couple of interesting lines of code involve calculating the total amount of an *OrderLine*, as shown in the following:

```
/// <summary>
/// Calculates the total.
/// </summary>
private void CalculateTotal()
{
    if (Discount > 0)
    {
        Total = Product.Price * Quantity * Discount;
    }
    else
    {
        Total = Product.Price * Quantity;
    }
}
```

As a constraint in the constructor of an *OrderLine*, we must already know how to build an *OrderLine* before creating one.

```
/// <summary>
/// Initializes a new instance of the <see cref="OrderLine"/> class.
/// </summary>
/// <param name="order">The order.</param>
/// <param name="product">The product.</param>
/// <param name="quantity">The quantity.</param>
/// <param name="discount">The discount.</param>
public OrderLine(Order order, Product product, int quantity, decimal discount)
```

```
    {
        this.Product = product;
        this.Quantity = quantity;
        this.Discount = discount;
        this.Order = order;
        CalculateTotal();
    }
```

The entire transaction is wrapped around the *AddProduct* method of an *Order* entity.

```
    /// <summary>
    /// Adds the product.
    /// </summary>
    /// <param name="product">The product.</param>
    /// <param name="quantity">The quantity.</param>
    /// <param name="discount">The discount.</param>
    public void AddProduct(Product product, int quantity, decimal discount = 0)
    {
        if (OrderLines == null)
        {
            OrderLines = new List<OrderLine>();
        }
        OrderLines.Add(new OrderLine(this, product, quantity, discount));
    }
```

The complete project code available with this book includes all the unit tests for the Domain, the factories for each Domain Entity and all the validation rules. To avoid printing numerous pages of C# code, the book itself includes only the highlighted steps of the Domain Model creation.

Summary

In this chapter, you created a basic Domain Model for a CRM application. This is the Business Context (not the business logic) for the application that you'll complete in the following chapters. You can easily extend this Domain by using a different approach or by adding new entities, such as those in the suggestions below:

- The *Product* should reference a *Magazine* or *Stock* that will keep the inventory and availability of the *Product* itself up to date.

- The *Approval* process used in the *Order* process should contact the corresponding *Customer* and *Employee* using their default address every time the status of the *Approval* changes.

For other improvements, we will use a specific Business Layer in Chapter 5, "The Business Layer," where you'll see how to implement custom rules and workflow for approving, rejecting, and completing an order.

Chapter 4
The Data Access Layer

After completing this chapter, you will be able to:

- Identify and choose the proper Object/Relational Mapper.
- Create a flexible Data Access Layer.
- Create a mapping with Entity Framework and with NHibernate.

Introduction

The Data Access Layer (DAL) abstracts data access and storage away from the rest of the application, providing a Separation of Concerns (SoC) that lets you separate the mechanics of data storage and retrieval from the use of the data within the application. This means that the application and data store can evolve more easily—or even be swapped out completely. However, the two are not completely decoupled; there is a "contract" between them which is designed so that the DAL provides access to the specific data (entities) that the application needs, regardless of how the underlying data is actually stored. The DAL allows you to write the application in terms of entities, which can be read and updated through the DAL. The DAL also enforces any business rules or business logic to ensure data integrity.

Whether you are planning to use a third-party library, an open-source framework, a more complex Object/Relational Mapper (O/RM), or an in-house DAL, you should always try to keep its use encapsulated in the DAL component itself. This means that the DAL should expose atomic methods that are able to execute queries and interact with the internal objects that compose the DAL without exposing these objects to the other layers. Another problem you might face when building a custom DAL is the mapping process. The DAL must provide a translation mechanism between the data model (the Domain Entities) that the application will use and the underlying data storage and schema. You can do this manually and simultaneously gain some benefits in terms of performance and customizability, or you could also employ an O/RM framework such as Microsoft Entity Framework or NHibernate (just to mention two) to make the translation more flexible and increase the level of standardization.

The use of a DAL in a Model View ViewModel (MVVM) application is not a mandatory requirement because the two architectural patterns are not interconnected; the DAL describes a way of layering the data access component while the MVVM describes a presentation design pattern. Usually, you would also add a DAL to an MVVM application to maintain a clean SoC and to increase the flexibility of the application. Ideally, the Domain Entities should support the interfaces and features that make them ideal Model classes for use in an

MVVM application (such as *INotifyPropertyChanged, IErrorInfo,* and so on) by breaking the concept of POCO objects. In the same way, a well-designed DAL allows the application to retrieve the Model that it needs for a particular screen and supports updating it.

Using a DAL in your application isolates the UI and the Domain from the database. The example MVVM application will have a structure composed of the Domain (Chapter 3, "The Domain Model"), the DAL (this chapter), the Business Layer (Chapter 5, "The Business Layer") and the UI Layer (Chapter 6, "The UI Layer with MVVM").

The Database and Stored Procedures

A Database Management System (DBMS) is a set of computer programs that controls the creation, maintenance, and use of a database.

In my opinion, the most dangerous thing you can do in a database is create stored pro-cedures (SPs). It's possible that many of you will not agree with me on this point. From a Domain-Driven Design (DDD) perspective, here's why SPs are evil—not only in an MVVM application that uses a Data Layer, but also for more generic Line of Business (LOB) applica-tions that have been layered to increase the testing surface and decrease the effort involved in maintenance.

The main purpose of using a Data Layer is to abstract the application away from the data storage by making the other layers unaware of the persistence mechanism used by the DAL. If the data storage uses SPs then this goal can be achieved—in fact, several O/RM implemen-tations provide full support for SPs. On the other hand, the main purpose of having a DAL is to avoid tight coupling between the C# code and the database, apart from the contract that you define as part of the DAL. As long as the database fulfills this contract, you don't need to care at all about exactly what the underlying implementation is. You create a mockup of the DAL so that you can test everything on the upstream side of it. Similarly, you can test any-thing on the downstream side of the DAL to ensure that the database is fulfilling its contract.

Ideally, you would not keep the application business logic inside an SP, because an SP's role should focus more on maintaining data integrity within the database. However, in practice, creating solid business logic and data integrity can be considered as two sides of the same coin. Testing the business logic stored inside an SP is a complex task, as are maintaining a database and securing a database. These concepts are well understood by database adminis-trators, and of course many organizations might not tolerate the costs of building and main-taining a database where all applications have to play by the rules to ensure data integrity and security, because that wouldn't be practical.

To help clarify why you should avoid the use of SPs and introduce a flexible DAL-O/RM combination in your applications, I've included few common arguments that I use with database administrators:

- **Maintenance**   SPs are not easy to maintain. When you change an SP, you often need to change its signature to include a new parameter. As a result of that change, every piece of code that uses that SP is invalid—but the DBMS doesn't offer a way to find the dependencies between an SP and the C# code that uses it.

- **Security**   In Microsoft SQL Server, you can define and grant granular access to a single field of a single row of a table, and that's pretty safe, but with a DAL application you can simply apply security through a Security Layer without worrying about authentication and authorization on the database side.

- **Performance**   Most modern O/RMs can generate execution plans and optimize the Dynamic SQL created by the DAL, which effectively ends the fantasy story that SPs are more efficient in terms of performance than dynamic SQL statements.

If you are still motivated to use SPs in your applications, you are of course free to do so. You should also consider that O/RMs such as NHibernate and Entity Framework are able to replace their auto-generated T-SQL code using some predesigned SPs that you might need to use if you have a legacy database.

Choosing an O/RM

An O/RM (also known as an Object-Relational Mapper) is a framework in charge of converting data between two disparate systems. One of these systems is usually an Object Model and the second one is a database object, such as a table or a view.

As you saw in Chapter 3, there are different ways to develop an application Domain. Based on whether you use an Active Record pattern or DDD, your O/RM will be configured differently.

The O/RM concept is an easy-to-understand but difficult-to-accomplish mechanism for persistence. It stores the instructions to map a Domain Object against one or more database objects in a *mapping dictionary*. Using this dictionary, the O/RM generates the necessary code to retrieve and store data from the database to the Domain Model and vice versa, on the fly. It usually also generates a ghost class of your Domain Model known as a *proxy*, which is an override of the Domain Model class specifically for the persistence aspect.

More than that, many O/RMs offer the ability to cache data, write transactions against the data store, and might even provide an object-oriented programming query language that is fully integrated with the Domain Ubiquitous Language, translated on demand to a Domain-Specific Language (DSL) understandable by the data store. Some O/RMs also offer the ability to switch between different databases, such as from SQL Server to Oracle, or from MySQL to IBM DB2.

The following list shows why it's so important to use an O/RM in an MVVM application:

- **Isolation**   You can completely isolate the Domain from the data store. This is a principal rule of a DDD application, and of course, for any LOB MVVM application.

- **Simplification**   O/RMs eliminate the need to write code to create, modify, and query database objects.

- **Improved Maintainability**   With an O/RM, you need to change only the Domain Model; the data store will be adapted automatically if you plan to use the O/RM to drive the maintenance of your database schema.

- **Domain Navigation**   It's not easy to understand how a database flow works just by reading the available table schema, but it's usually quite easy to read a UML diagram of a Domain Model to understand how the application has been designed. If you use an O/RM, the Domain will be your only blueprint. Of course, in this case you can achieve the same *goal* using a custom DAL; it is important that behind that there is a Domain Model.

- **Features**   My motto is, why re-invent the wheel? O/RMs offer features such as caching, transactional capabilities, concurrency checking, and so forth.

That's probably enough. O/RMs are cool and shiny—but not all that glitters is gold. For example, an O/RM generates dynamic SQL as needed, so it probably isn't a good fit with some specific architectural designs. Here are two more considerations:

- **Learning Curve Degrades**   It's been my experience that there's a problem with the learning curve, especially with an O/RM or a technology such as XAML. If you don't know how to use these properly, you can easily end up using them the wrong way, resulting in the worst outcome from using the products.

- **Large Bulk Operations**   While most modern O/RMs are able to execute bulk operations, they don't always choose the best possible method to do them. For example, truncating a table is far more efficient than clearing an *IList<Employee>*, which, when executed by an O/RM, is often translated to a set of *DELETE* commands.

There are several types of O/RMs on the market that range from reliable, to semi-reliable, to only for newbies. In the next sections, I will show the most reliable O/RMs and—based purely on my experience—when you should use one instead of another.

Microsoft Entity Framework

Microsoft introduced the Entity Framework quite some time ago. At the time of this writing, Entity Framework is at version 4 and is delivered with Microsoft .NET Framework 4.0.

The latest version of this O/RM covers all the requirements of a standard O/RM, including lazy loading, persistence ignorance, a UI designer, and a query translator that allows developers to use the well-known LINQ syntax.

You can connect the Entity Framework to various databases, including SQL Server, Oracle, DB2, and more. This capability, plus the availability of a graphical tool to design the mapping, makes the Entity Framework an easy O/RM to learn and use. However, it's probably still less powerful than other O/RMs available on the market.

Entity Framework is composed of a layer that capitalizes on existing Microsoft ADO.NET technology, which makes learning Entity Framework syntax and usage easy for Microsoft developers who already have an ADO.NET background. Figure 4-1 displays the basic structure of Entity Framework 4.

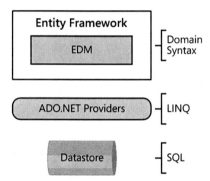

FIGURE 4-1 The Microsoft Entity Framework layered structure.

To create a new Data Model using Entity Framework 4, you need to understand what the available models are and why you should create one type rather than another. The Entity Framework shown in Figure 4-2 currently allows you to create three different models:

- **ADO.NET Entity Data Model**   Using this model, the Entity Framework will create a new empty Domain Model. You have the option of creating the initial model from an existing database (the "database-first" approach) or creating an empty Domain Model that you will later map to a database.

- **ADO.NET Entity Object Generator**   Using this option, you can create a strongly-typed Object Context and persistence-aware classes starting from an existing Entity Framework domain by using the Text Templating (TT) feature of Microsoft Visual Studio 2010.

> **Note** In Visual Studio, a text template is a mixture of text blocks and control logic that can generate a text file. The control logic is written as fragments of program code in Microsoft Visual C# or Microsoft Visual Basic. The generated file can be text of any kind, such as a webpage, or a resource file, or program source code in any language. Text templates can be used at runtime to produce part of the output of an application. They can also be used for code generation, in which the templates help build part of the source code of an application.

- **ADO.NET Self-Tracking Entity**   You use this option to generate entity types that have the ability to record changes on scalar and complex property values, and on reference and collection navigation properties, independent of the Entity Framework.

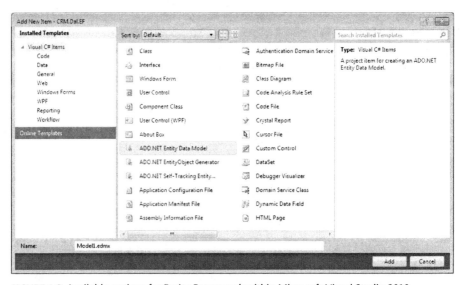

FIGURE 4-2 Available options for Entity Framework within Microsoft Visual Studio 2010.

Right now, Entity Framework version 4 is still lacking in its implementation of the POCO concept. In fact, if you have an existing Domain Model such as the one created in Chapter 3, the only solution is to create a manual mapping for each entity, bypassing the power of the integrated Entity Framework designer. Alternatively, you would need to use the Entity Framework designer to create a proxy entity for each Domain Entity.

Here are the pros and cons of using Entity Framework for your data mapping:

Pros

- Entity Framework is easy to learn, easy to use, and has rich wizard and UI designers that allow you to create a model from an existing database with just a few clicks.

- It is fully integrated with the .NET LINQ query language.

- It's a Microsoft product that will benefit from continued updates and enhancements, and it is probably the most reliable in terms of lifecycle.

- Entity Framework is perfect for a database-first approach because it has a powerful T4 code generator that can generate a full Domain Model starting from an existing database.

Cons

- Entity Framework forces you to use LINQ to Entities, an extension of LINQ designed for Entity Framework with a somewhat different syntax than the original LINQ provider.

- It lacks the flexible support for lazy load and POCO concepts that are present in other O/RMs.

- The SQL it generates is still not perfect, and in some situations, the performance is unacceptable.

With Entity Framework, you can write mapping files two ways. One way is to decorate your POCO objects using Entity Framework attributes, specifying the SQL data type, the field name in the data store, and the validation rules for each property. Here's an example of this approach:

```
public class Book
{
    [Key]
    public string ISBN { get; set; }

    [StringLength(256)]
    public string Title { get; set; }

    public string AuthorSSN { get; set; }

    [RelatedTo(RelatedProperty="Books", Key="AuthorSSN", RelatedKey="SSN")]
    public Person Author { get; set; }
}
```

The second way is to use three available XML files to specify the database mappings, the entity mappings, and the relationship mappings, as demonstrated here:

```
<Association Name="CustomerOrders">
  <End Type="ExampleModel.Customer" Role="Customer" Multiplicity="1" />
  <End Type="ExampleModel.Order" Role="Order" Multiplicity="*">
        <OnDelete Action="Cascade" />
  </End>
  <ReferentialConstraint>
      <Principal Role="Customer">
         <PropertyRef Name="Id" />
      </Principal>
      <Dependent Role="Order">
          <PropertyRef Name="CustomerId" />
       </Dependent>
  </ReferentialConstraint>
</Association>
```

NHibernate

Started in 2005, NHibernate is an open-source O/RM for .NET that is derived from the successful open-source O/RM for Java called Hibernate. It is now one of the most popular and most-used O/RMs in the open-source community; it has well-established community support and numerous plug-in and code generators.

The concept behind NHibernate is pretty simple: you create your POCO-compliant Domain Model, and then you decide how to map it against a database. You can use an existing database (the database-first approach) or create a new one (the domain-first approach).

NHibernate has all the characteristics of a professional O/RM, such as persistence ignorance, lazy load and fetch strategies, a complex query language, full support for LINQ, and many more features. You can see an overview of this product at *http://nhforge.com*, the official NHibernate community.

Figure 4-3 shows the structure of NHibernate version 3 (the latest version as of this writing). At the top of the diagram sits the Domain Model, which is totally unaware of the O/RM; then the mapping, which can be accomplished using a separate assembly composed of either XML files or C# classes; and finally, the core NHibernate engine, which translates the mapping files into proxies that are able to speak with the targeted data store. NHibernate handles this architecture using the *session object*, which is a contextual object that holds the status of the Domain Model objects and tracks their changes so that developers can determine whether an entity is new or already exists, and whether it has been modified. All these steps are clear and can be executed using a transaction (Database Transaction) pattern.

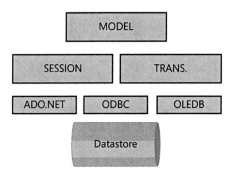

FIGURE 4-3 The NHibernate architecture

Pros

■ NHibernate is extremely powerful and flexible. You can execute SQL calls directly from the O/RM session, access the OLEDB/ODBC connection object, manage transactions, and configure stored procedures and views.

- NHibernate is an open-source product with a very large community. It thus benefits from extensive documentation, such as easy-to-find e-books, blogs, code samples, and sample projects on the Internet.

- You can find a number of free plug-ins for NHibernate that assist in tasks from configuring your domain mapping, to writing LINQ queries, to using a GUI designer inside Visual Studio.

- Again, NHibernate is an open-source project, which makes it highly customizable and configurable. You can obtain the latest build and configure it—and even change the core code if you want or need to. Beyond that, NHibernate has a very powerful tracing engine; you can monitor the dynamic SQL and the mappings it creates.

Cons

- It's an open-source product—and yes I realize that I've just been expounding the virtues of an open-source project. But the flip side to open-source applications is that they can be a big risk, because there's no guaranteed support or any warranty that the product will be available as long as you need it.

- It has a steep learning curve. At the beginning, NHibernate is not an easy solution. The configuration is extremely complex (especially if you choose the XML method), and the core engine has thousands of options and methods that can give you poor performance if used incorrectly.

- It works better with the custom SQL generated by the engine. It is not intended to be used with customized SQL statements or for bulk operations.

The code example that follows shows the classic mapping used by NHibernate and by its Java parent Hibernate. Specifically, the example shows an XML file with an .hbm.xml extension. Everything is defined using a specific XML format, based on three main .xsd files that you can easily import into Visual Studio—after which, Visual Studio will provide custom IntelliSense.

```xml
<?xml version="1.0" encoding="utf-8" ?>
<hibernate-mapping xmlns="urn:nhibernate-mapping-2.2"
  namespace="QuickStart" assembly="QuickStart">

  <class name="Cat" table="Cat">
    <id name="Id">
      <generator class="identity" />
    </id>

    <property name="Name">
      <column name="Name" length="16" not-null="true" />
    </property>
    <property name="Sex" />
    <many-to-one name="Mate" />
```

```
  <bag name="Kittens">
    <key column="mother_id" />
      <one-to-many class="Cat" />
    </bag>
  </class>
</hibernate-mapping>
```

FluentNHibernate is another tool you might want to consider that lets you write mapping files using C#. FluentNHibernate is an open-source plug-in, available at *http://fluentnhibernate. org*. In the next section, you'll see a couple of examples that demonstrate how it works.

The team at NHibernate has just released a major new version of NHibernate, 3.0, which will be available in RTM form at the beginning of 2011. In this version, the team has added full support for LINQ syntax plus an internal C# fluent mapping called confORM. No preview of this plug-in is available yet, but the code should look something like the following example:

```
var orm = new ObjectRelationalMapper();
orm.TablePerClass<Animal>();
orm.TablePerClass<User>();
orm.TablePerClass<StateProvince>();
orm.TablePerClassHierarchy<Zoo>();
orm.ManyToMany<Human, Human>();
orm.OneToOne<User, Human>();
orm.PoidStrategies.Add(new NativePoidPattern());
```

Other O/RMs for .NET

Entity Framework and NHibernate are probably the most commonly used O/RMs in the .NET world—possibly because both are free. Entity Framework ships with the .NET Framework and NHibernate is open source.

If you are looking for a code generator tool that also acts as an O/RM, you might want to consider a third-party O/RM. Most of these are not free. The following table attempts to summarize the pros and cons of two of these products:

Name	URL	Pros	Cons
Subsonic	*http://subsonicproject.com*	Active Record Auto-generate code	Open Source, Not flexible
Genome	*http://www.genom-e.com*	Flexible Auto-generate code	Expensive, Sparse documentation

The Unit of Work

If you plan to write your DAL using an O/RM, you won't need to put a lot of effort into writing custom SQL code and custom transactional code to save or retrieve entities. On the other hand, you do need a solid "orchestrator" which will be in charge of entity status. For example, you need to know whether an entity is new, or whether a requested entity is already in memory or needs to be retrieved from the data store.

Martin Fowler introduced the concept of the Unit of Work (UoW) (see Chapter 2, "Design Patterns"). The UoW is in charge of maintaining a list of objects affected by a business transaction and coordinating writing out changes and resolving concurrency problems.

Each of the O/RMs discussed in the previous section have a UoW concept at their core. NHibernate uses the *Session* and *ITransaction* objects, Entity Framework uses the *ObjectContext* class, and basic LinQToSQL uses the *DataContext*. These are implemented and work differently, but their main goals are the same. The following code displays the basic concept of a UoW:

```
Public IUnitOfWork<T>
{
    void MarkDirty<T> (T entity);
    void MarkNew<T> (T entity);
    void MarkDeleted<T> (T entity);
    void Commit();
    void Rollback();
}
```

The main concept here is that the UoW takes care of entity status. The only thing you need to remember to do is to mark an entity with the specific status and then *Commit* or *Rollback* the business transaction. The next pseudo-code example shows how this works over a complete transaction using the UoW pattern:

```
var unitOfWork = Container.Resolve<IUnitOfWork>(); //IoC to retrieve the IUnitOfWork
var customer = Factory.CreateCustomer();
var order = Factory.CreateOrder();
customer.Orders.Add(order);
try {
    unitOfWork.MarkNew(customer); //mark the new entity
    unitOfWork.Commit();  //commit the changes to the database
} catch(Exception ex) {
    unitOfWork.Rollback();  //rollback if an error occurs
}
```

If you keep this pattern in the DAL, you don't need to implement a custom DAL for each O/RM that you plan to use. For example, you might have an application composed of two DALs: one is the Entity Framework, and the other is a more complex DAL that uses NHibernate. In this case, you might only need to implement the *IUnitOfWork* interface in two different ways, using the most appropriate one for each DAL, without having to change the code of the *UnitOfWork* itself.

I've seen the *UnitOfWork* over engineered in many projects. For example, I've seen a *UnitOfWork* implementation that was able to retrieve data, execute SQL statements, and more. At that point, of course, it isn't really the *UnitOfWork* pattern any longer; it's the Repository pattern (you'll explore more about this in the next sections). Remember that the only purpose of the *UnitOfWork* is to keep the state of a set of business objects for a related business transaction.

Lifecycle of a UoW

Another important point is the lifecycle of your UoW. The lifecycle depends on the type of application that you are writing. For example, a business transaction that involves a Windows Presentation Foundation (WPF) client application might be very different than a business transaction that happens in a more web-oriented Silverlight application.

In the classic MVVM pattern, I usually like to associate the lifecycle of a *UnitOfWork* to the corresponding View/ViewModel association. That way, everything that happens in the ViewModel is covered by a UoW transaction. If I need to work on a web application, I try to get help from the *HttpContext* object, and store the UoW within it. But remember, everything depends on the type of application that you are writing; the lifecycle of the UoW is context sensitive.

The Oracle guide for Database Transactions (*http://download.oracle.com/docs/cd/B14099_19/ web.1012/b15901/xactions002.htm#i1132715*) defines the UoW as a business context that opens a transaction as soon as the business activity begins and controls this activity by committing or rolling back that transaction. It's up to you to determine when the business activity is complete and when you need to commit any changes.

Identify a Business Transaction

In an MVVM application, the business transaction is usually strictly related to the View/ ViewModel coupling, but some cases might not satisfy this requirement. For example, you might have a main View that displays all the available customers. At the same time, you might have a Command that allows users to add, modify, or remove a customer from that list.

Because many views include subviews, there is usually a hierarchy of view models, as well; the association between a transaction is usually at the screen level, which in this case might be composed of more than one child View/ViewModel coupling. Figure 4-4 displays a practical example in WPF.

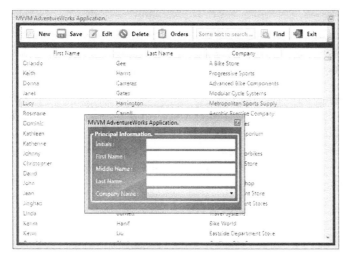

FIGURE 4-4 A sample WPF MVVM Master Detail's application.

You can see that there are two types of business transactions here. The first one occurs as soon as the main view loads. At that point, you call the UoW and retrieve all the available data from the data store. You then display this data in the View using your ViewModel. This transaction is completed as soon as the data is displayed in the View.

The second transaction might happen any time you add, modify, or delete a customer. This transaction is pretty simple but challenging at the same time. For example, clicking the Add Customer command creates a new View/ViewModel with an associated UoW that might or might not be committed, depending on a specific business logic. In the following example, the persistence is committed in the command call. Clicking the Save command adds a new customer to the current session of the UoW. At that point, you should commit the transaction and refresh the main ViewModel. Is this a unique transaction or is it a set of transactions? Well, in business transaction terms, this is just one transaction that includes the following steps:

```
Using (var uow = Container.Resolve<IUnitOfWork>())
{
   try{
      uow.BeginTransaction();
      var customer = CustomerViewModel.GetModel();
      uow.SaveOrUpdate(customer);
      MainViewModel.Refresh();
      uow.Commit();
   }catch(Exception ex){
      uow.Rollback();
      MainViewModel.Refresh();
   }
}
```

The previous pseudo-code starts by getting a *Customer* entity from the *CustomerViewModel*, and then it tries to add or update this entity. Next, it refreshes the *MainViewModel*. If something goes wrong, the code rolls back the entire transaction and refreshes the *MainViewModel*—which should not display the new customer because the transaction failed.

In conclusion, the business transaction handled in a UoW should not be considered the same as a simple database transaction; instead, consider it as a set of operations that will accomplish one or more business "steps." NHibernate's *ITransaction* object, for example, can handle multiple SQL calls, executing them only when you call the Commit command. At the same time, based on your configuration, it will update the current session, and of course, the list of available customers to match the changes made through the UI.

The Repository Pattern

In the previous section, you saw the core of a DAL, the UoW. Unfortunately, with the basic UoW pattern, you can only add, remove, or update an entity and execute a business transaction, but to have a complete DAL, you need more than that. You need to be able to retrieve a set of entities, to lazy-load related child and parent entities, and to be able to query and page results without affecting database performance. For these and other business requirements of the DAL, you need to use the Repository pattern.

Martin Fowler first introduced the concept of the Repository pattern in his book, *Patterns of Enterprise Application Architecture* (see Chapter 2). A repository should act as an in-memory collection of entities, and it should facilitate the query and retrieval processes for these entities without affecting database performance.

A basic repository should support adding and removing entities, and updating existing entities. It should also provide an easy way to retrieve and query them. The following pseudo-code displays a common Repository pattern:

```
interface ICustomerRepository
{
    void AddCustomer(Customer customer);
    void RemoveCustomer(Customer customer);
    void UpdateCustomer(Customer customer);

    IQueryable<Customer> GetCustomers();
    Customer GetCustomer(object primaryKey);
}
```

Using the following "contract," you can implement a concrete *CustomerRepository* that will be able to execute any type of Create, Read, Update, or Delete (CRUD) operation against the data store using the UoW. Of course, each of these operations might be included in one or more business transactions. In particular, note the *GetCustomers* method, which, as you might have noticed, doesn't return a "real" collection at all; it returns an *IQueryable<T>* collection. That's because *IQueryable* is the only collection type that is able to execute a call to the database when you access only one of the items of the collection. That means you can apply additional LINQ filters to the collection before the final call to the database executes. For example, if you write the following code, and the O/RM is Entity Framework or NHibernate:

```
var repository = Container.Resolve<ICustomerRepository>();
var customers = repository.GetCustomers()
                .Where(x => x.Company == "Microsoft)
                .OrderBy(x => x.FirstName);
// call to the Db
customers.ToList();
```

the final T-SQL generated from our O/RM, if well configured, will be something like this:

```
SELECT * FROM
TBL_CUSTOMER C WHERE C.COMPANY = 'Microsoft'
ORDER BY C.FIRSTNAME
```

You can see the *IQueryable<T>* collection type analyzed in more detail at *http://msdn. microsoft.com/en-us/library/system.linq.iqueryable.aspx*. *IQueryable<T>* is part of the *System. Linq* namespace, and not a part of the *System.Collections* namespace like other collections available in .NET. Of course, to use it properly, you must be sure that your O/RM has full support for LINQ or one of its providers.

To keep this concept general, you might consider using .NET generics and creating a more generic Repository pattern contract, such as the following:

```
Interface IRepository<T>
{
    void Add(T entity);
    void Remove(T entity);
    void Update(T entity);

    T Get(object primaryKey);
    IQueryable<T> GetEntities();
}
```

This code creates a more generic contract that we can recycle throughout our applications, and that—in conjunction with a generic UoW—makes a very flexible and reusable DAL. Later in this chapter, you'll build simple *UoW* and *IRepository* classes using generics and see how easy it is to plug these two powerful patterns into the same MVVM project by using two different O/RMs.

A sample implementation of a generic Repository should look like this:

```
public GenericRepository<T> : IRepository<T>
{
    private IUnitOfWork uow;

    public GenericRepository()
    {
        this.uow = Container.Resolve<uow>();
    }

    public void Add<T> (T entity){
        try
        {
            uow.BeginTransaction();
            uow.Add(entity);
            uow.Commit();
        }catch (Exception ex){
            uow.Rollback();
        }
    }
}
```

Test-Driven Development: The Data Layer

In Chapter 2, I stressed how important Test-Driven Development (TDD) is and why you need to introduce it at the beginning of the development process. Of course, the Data Layer also needs to be tested.

To test the Data Layer, you should follow two different directions, depending on the composition of the DAL. The first step is to test the mapping against the O/RM; you need to be sure that the entity is mapped properly in the O/RM, and that each field is mapped to the appropriate field in the database. For example, you don't want the *FirstName* property of the *Customer* entity mapped to the *LastName* field of the Customer's table.

To test the mapping, depending on the O/RM you are using, you should follow a few simple steps. First, you want to ensure that when you create and save a new entity, for example, a *Customer* entity, that the values are persisted properly in the database. To accomplish this test, you simply need to create a new entity, save it, retrieve it, and then check it against a static value.

```
public void CanSaveFirstName()
{
    var firstName = "John";
    var customer = Factory.Create<Customer>();
    customer.FirstName = firstName;
    GenericRepository<Customer>.Add(customer);
    var expected = GenericRepository<Customer>.Get(customer.PrimaryKey);
    Assert.AreEquals(expected.FirstName, firstName);
}
```

Such operations can be time-consuming, but are necessary when you need to be 100% sure that the mapping has been done properly and that no property is missing. If you are using Entity Framework, you might not need to execute this set of steps, because the UI designer makes it easy to see when the mapping has been done properly, especially if you generate your domain starting from an existing database.

If you're planning to build a domain-first application, and you're writing the mapping for your POCO objects manually, you must guarantee the mapping validity by using the TDD approach, which can be very expensive in terms of time and resources.

You should also remember that the data store used for the TDD should not be the same one you use for the final application, or you will end up with a set of "fake" records in the production data store.

The second type of tests should be executed only when you are not auto-mapping your model and if you are specifying different names for the data store fields than the names used for the entity fields. In my company, for example, we work with very private information, so we can't use actual names in the database fields, because that would be a potential security breach. To accomplish this, we write tables and fields using numeric mappings, as shown in the following table:

Table	Field	Description
Tbl801	801_1	Id
Tbl801	801_2	FirstName

This type of naming can be difficult to decode and is also prone to error. For this reason when I create a mapping class or XML for a specific entity, I need to be sure that the mapping is done properly—and the only way to do that is to execute a *SELECT* against the data store and then check that the mapped field on my entity is the same as on the data store.

If you're planning to work with NHibernate, you might consider using a very handy tool for writing the mapping in C#, called FluentNHibernate (available at *http://fluentnhibernate.org*). This tool makes extensive use of lambda expressions to create your mapping files. It's also a very useful TDD component that you can use to verify correct mapping and that the mapping works on the data store.

The following example shows how FluentNHibernate lets you write "fluent" mapping files:

```
public class CatMap : ClassMap<Cat>
{
  public CatMap()
  {
    Id(x => x.Id);
    Map(x => x.Name)
      .Length(16)
      .Not.Nullable();
    Map(x => x.Sex);
    References(x => x.Mate);
    HasMany(x => x.Kittens);
  }
}
```

The next code example shows you how to test your mapping against a data store using the FluentNHibernate component. The code creates a new *Employee* entity, persists it to the database, and then verifies that the entity has been persisted properly.

```
[Test]
public void CanCorrectlyMapEmployee()
{
    new PersistenceSpecification<Employee>(session)
        .CheckProperty(c => c.Id, 1)
        .CheckProperty(c => c.FirstName, "John")
        .CheckProperty(c => c.LastName, "Doe")
        .VerifyTheMappings();
}
```

One final consideration: remember that the domain mapping for a normal MVVM application happens just once during the entire lifecycle of the application. Of course, you will need to change and modify the Domain and the data store during the application's lifetime, but the main schema should not change. A good TDD layer for the DAL will guarantee that every change you make to the Domain will be properly reflected to the corresponding data store.

Building a Distributed Data Layer with RIA and WCF

What you've seen so far is fine if your DAL is written in C# or Visual Basic .NET, and if it's used by a "normal" .NET application that uses the common CLR, such as a WPF Client application. This means that you can write your custom and generic DAL once and reuse it repeatedly for your WPF application, for your ASP.NET application, or for a simple Windows Service application. If you are using a three-tier approach, the concept becomes more complex. This is because you will need to add an additional abstraction using a Windows Communication Foundation (WCF) or a web service technology that will provide the atomic methods to call the DAL stored at the application server level.

Unfortunately, as soon as you jump into a Silverlight application, the process fails, because Silverlight runs under a smaller and less powerful version of the CLR designed solely for Silverlight, which is not (currently) able to run DLLs compiled for the Common CLR. Fortunately, the solution is not to re-compile all your layers to satisfy Silverlight's requirements; otherwise, every time you change something in the Domain or in the DAL you would also need to recompile everything just for your Silverlight application.

Microsoft introduced the WCF RIA Service for Silverlight. The concept carried by this service is simple but very potent. WCF is a powerful technology that allows you to communicate between layers using the Simple Object Access Protocol (SOAP) protocol (like a web service) and to share data and data structures between a Domain and layers by using XML. You can capitalize on WCF RIA Services to share your DAL and your Domain compiled for the Common CLR with a Silverlight application (see Figure 4-5), without the need to recompile everything for each change.

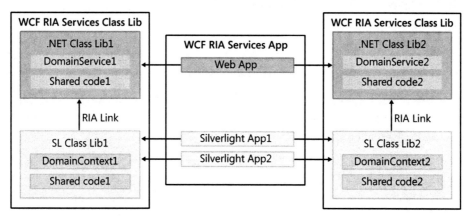

FIGURE 4-5 The core structure of WCF RIA Services.

In Figure 4-5, you can see that there are two distinct boundaries, one of which is the Silverlight application itself along with a "clone" of the application logic, shared by a web service, and a second boundary composed of the Data Layer and the database, also shared using the WCF Service. In this case, there are at least two different tiers: one is the MVVM Silverlight application, and one is the data tier, composed of the data store and the Data Layer.

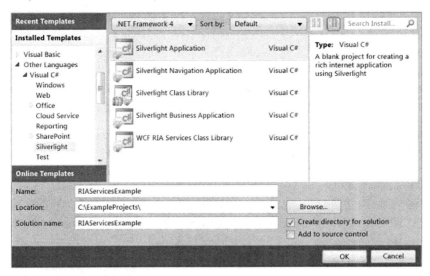

FIGURE 4-6 How to create a Silverlight Application that includes WCF RIA Services.

You can use WCF RIA Services in your WPF applications if you want, but they were originally designed to satisfy the problem of Silverlight generating code only for the Silverlight CLR.

To create a WCF RIA Application, you need a base Silverlight Client application. This application will have a Silverlight project and an ASP.NET or ASP.NET MVC website that hosts the compiled Silverlight application.

After creating the base Silverlight Client, you need to add a new WCF RIA Service to the web application, as shown in Figure 4-6. At this point, you are able to share the DAL, Domain, and anything else you need from your Common CLR to the Silverlight application. Figure 4-7 summarizes these steps, and shows you how simple it is to use and how simple it is to share a Domain across a Silverlight application.

> **Note** To be precise, you'd usually use this wizard when creating a Domain Model based exactly on the database schema of the table you choose, which is not typical of what you would do in a real LOB application.

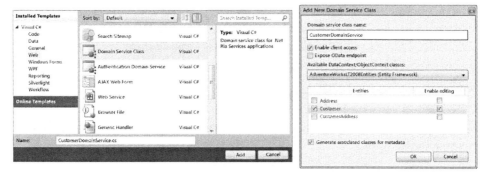

FIGURE 4-7 Two easy steps to add an existing Domain to a WCF RIA Service.

Having added the references to the Silverlight application, you are ready to query your Domain using your existing DAL from the Silverlight code. Because RIA Services has full support for XAML code, this is a very good combination for the MVVM pattern, as well.

The following code loads some data into the *ViewModel* and binds it to a grid in a Silverlight View:

```
public class GridViewModel : ViewModel
    {
        private CustomerDomainContext customerContext = new CustomerDomainContext();
        public LoadOperation<Customer> VMDataSource;
        public GridViewModel()
        {
            InitializeView();
            VMDataSource = this. customerContext.Load(
                this.customerContext.GetCustomersByLastNameLetterQuery(LetterValue.Text),
                CustomerLoadedCallback, null);
        }
    }
//XAML

<Page.Resources>
 <vm:GridViewModel />
</Page.Resources>
<myGrid:DataGrid DataSource="{Binding Path=VMDataSource}" ...
```

Note WCF RIA Services work well with O/RM, Entity Framework, and NHibernate.

This listing introduced a *CustomerDomainContext*—a custom class that inherits from the *DomainContext* class and is created by the WCF RIA Services Wizard. A domain context class is generated in the client project for every domain service in the server project. You call methods on the domain context class that correspond to the domain service method that you want to use.

If you want to keep an eye on WCF RIA Services, Microsoft has an official website for this technology (*http://www.silverlight.net/getstarted/riaservices*) where you can find a lot of useful code, samples, and tutorials. If you have an existing DAL and you are planning to build your next LOB application using Silverlight, you should definitely consider using WCF RIA Services to save time and work.

Of course, if you plan to use this approach, you will need to consider additional issues that accompany the SOA approach, such as records concurrency, data latency, and bottlenecks across the network.

Sample Code: The CRM Data Access Layer

In the Sample Code section of Chapter 3, we created the Domain Model for the CRM example application, which is composed of two main groups of entities: the *Person* entity and the *Order* entity. In this chapter, we'll map that Domain to a database using two different O/RMs: Entity Framework and NHibernate.

A Flexible *IUnitOfWork* Interface

Before creating the domain mapping, you need to create the basic *IUnitOfWork* interface, which will be used throughout the layers of the MVVM application. The class diagram in Figure 4-8 illustrates an *IUnitOfWork* interface that is very close to the UoW explained earlier in this chapter. The UoW will expose the three principal commands to change the status of an entity (*Create, Update, Delete*) as well as functions to execute these commands in a transaction context.

The UoW will be specific to each O/RM because Entity Framework uses the *ObjectContext*, while NHibernate uses the *ISession* interface. For this reason, the *IUnitOfWork* will not expose the real *DataContext*, only the basic commands needed to execute the SQL statements. The application uses the *ISessionFactory* interface for the same reason; depending on the O/RM in use, we will create a specific concrete *UnitOfWork* that will have an O/RM-specific *DataContext*.

Finally, you'll need a generic *Repository* that will perform the CRUD operations in a transactional context. The *Repository* will expose the current *IUnitOfWork* so that we will be able to execute specific commands as well as the predefined CRUD operations available through the *Repository*.

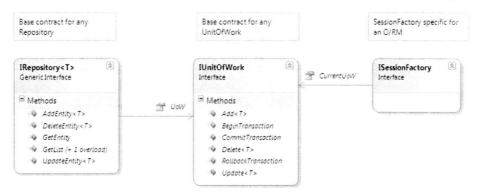

FIGURE 4-8 The CRM.Dal abstract layer: the basic layer for any DAL.

You also need to create two additional layers: one for Entity Framework, and one for NHibernate. As mentioned earlier, this step is required because you can choose which O/RM you want to use, but you can't apply the same concrete *UnitOfWork* to two different O/RMs, because they manage entity persistence and the data context in different ways. The final result should look like the diagram in Figure 4-9. Remember that all the code mentioned in this book is available in the CRM example application included in the downloadable companion content for this book.

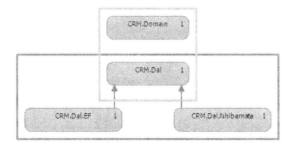

FIGURE 4-9 The CRM Domain with the complete Data Layer.

Figure 4-9 shows that the Domain is totally unaware of the persistence technique in use. At the same time, the abstract Data Layer that you will use in your MVVM application doesn't know about the concrete implementation.

Mapping the Domain Model Using Entity Framework

Using Entity Framework, you can develop a Domain using two different DDD approaches: domain-first or database-first. As discussed in Chapter 3, you should avoid the database-first approach unless you are restricted to a specific legacy database. Because the CRM application is new, we will not be bound to a specific database schema, so we will use the domain-first approach here.

Before .NET Framework 4.0, you were not able to create a complete POCO Domain and plug it into a new Entity Framework model, but with version 4, you can now accomplish this task without the need to rewrite everything. Unfortunately, Entity Framework requires a set of proxy classes that act as mappers for the POCO Domain Entities. Therefore, you need to implement the same model you have in the Domain in the Entity Framework designer. This mandatory requirement causes a major problem; Entity Framework needs to know how to perform lazy loading and how to persist a POCO entity. Because the entity is POCO, the only way to do that is to create a proxy that overrides the POCO entity with the specific configuration for the database.

To start, create a new project and name it **CRM.Dal.EF.** This will be a concrete implementation of the Data Layer for Entity Framework. Next, add these three references: *CRM.DAL* (our base data layer), *System.Data.Entity* (Entity Framework) and *System.ComponentModel. Composition* (MEF for the Plug-In design).

Now, add a new empty .edmx file (ADO.NET Entity Model). You need to create the same entities that exist in your basic domain. This step is pretty frustrating and overly time-consuming, but to keep your domain POCO unaware of the Entity Framework, this is the only solution available right now. The final result should be similar to Figure 4-10.

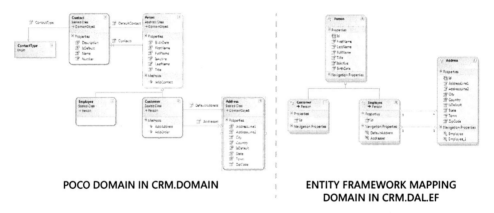

POCO DOMAIN IN CRM.DOMAIN   ENTITY FRAMEWORK MAPPING
                                             DOMAIN IN CRM.DAL.EF

FIGURE 4-10 Class diagrams comparison: POCO Domain versus Entity Framework Domain.

I have found some custom tools at *www.codeplex.com* that might help you to generate your custom Entity Framework mapping diagram from an existing POCO Domain. Of course, the best fit for this type of approach is to generate your Entity Framework Model from an existing database and then build proxies for your Domain Model. In this chapter, you saw the pros and cons of this O/RM. You should not use Entity Framework if you plan to keep a Domain Model totally POCO because the current release (CTP 4) still lacks a mapping process between Entity Framework proxies and POCO Domain Entities.

Creating a Concrete DAL for Entity Framework

The next step is to create a proxy *ObjectContext* that will be able to persist the POCO entities. The following code maps each Entity Framework proxy entity to its corresponding *CRM.*
Domain entity. To do this you must add a reference to the *CRM.DAL.EF* layer that points to
the *CRM.Domain*. You will not recycle this part of the DAL because it is specific to the sample
MVVM application for this specific Domain.

```
namespace CRM.Dal.EF
{
    public class CRMObjectContext : ObjectContext
    {
        public CRMObjectContext(string connectionString) : base(connectionString)
        {
                /// <summary>
                /// Gets or sets the employees.
                /// </summary>
                /// <value>The employees.</value>
                public ObjectSet<Employee> Employees { get; set; }

                /// <summary>
                /// Gets or sets the customers.
                /// </summary>
                /// <value>The customers.</value>
                public ObjectSet<Customer> Customers { get; set; }
        }
    }
}
```

Now that you have the *ObjectContext*, you can start to implement the concrete DAL for the
Entity Framework side. The first class you need to implement is, of course, the *UnitOfWork*,
which will inherit from *CRM.DAL.IUnitOfWork*. You need to instruct MEF that you're using a
plug-in *IUnitOfWork* by adding the *[Export]* attribute to the concrete *UnitOfWork* implementation, as shown in the following code:

```
[Export(typeof(IUnitOfWork))]
public class UnitOfWork : IUnitOfWork
{
    private ObjectContext orm;

    /// <summary>
    /// Initializes a new instance of the <see cref="UnitOfWork"/> class.
    /// </summary>
    /// <param name="orm">The orm.</param>
    public UnitOfWork(ObjectContext orm)
    {
        this.orm = orm;
    }
```

In the UoW constructor you will inject the current *ObjectContext*, which is the proxy used for
your Domain Model.

The next short code example shows a simple *Add* method. Basically, you must add the entity to the *ObjectContext*. Then the *CommitTransaction* method will try to update the Entity Framework session in a transactional context. If the *Add* operation fails, Entity Framework doesn't need a rollback method, because it will automatically roll back the entities' status:

```
/// <summary>
/// Adds the specified entity.
/// </summary>
/// <typeparam name="T"></typeparam>
/// <param name="entity">The entity.</param>
public void Add<T>(T entity)
{
    try
    {
        this.orm.AddObject(EntitySetName, entity);
    }
    catch (Exception ex)
    {
        throw new Exception(string.Format(
          "An error occurred during the Add Entity.\r\n{0}", ex.Message));
    }
}
/// <summary>
/// Commits the transaction.
/// </summary>
public void CommitTransaction()
{
    try
    {
        if (tx == null)
        {
            throw new TransactionException(
                "The current transaction is not started!");
        }
        orm.SaveChanges(false);
        tx.Complete();
        orm.AcceptAllChanges();
    }
    catch (Exception ex)
    {
        throw new Exception(string.Format(
          "An error occurred during the Commit transaction.\r\n{0}", ex.Message));
    }
    finally
    {
        tx.Dispose();
    }
}
```

The second class you will implement is the generic *Repository* that inherits from *CRM.DAL. IRepository* and that exposes all the available methods from the *IRepository* interface. The *Repository* will also have an *Export* attribute so that you can use MEF in the MVVM layer to load the selected O/RM on the fly.

```
[Export(typeof(IRepository))]
public class Repository : IRepository
{
    [Import]
    private IUnitOfWork uow;

    /// <summary>
    /// Adds the entity.
    /// </summary>
    /// <typeparam name="T"></typeparam>
    /// <param name="entity">The entity.</param>
    /// <returns></returns>
    public T AddEntity<T>(T entity)
    {
        try
        {
            uow.BeginTransaction();
            uow.Add(entity);
            uow.CommitTransaction();
            return entity;
        }
        catch (Exception ex)
        {
            uow.RollbackTransaction();
            throw new Exception(string.Format(
                "An error occurred during the Add Entity method.", ex));
        }
    }
}
```

Note that the code marks the private field *IUnitOfWork* with the *[Import]* attribute. MEF will use this attribute to realize the corresponding mapped concrete *UnitOfWork* at run-time when you create a new instance of the *Repository* class. All the other methods of the Repository should be implemented similarly: you open a transaction, call the corresponding *UnitOfWork* method, and then call *CommitTransaction* or *RollbackTransaction* at the end.

That completes the *UnitOfWork* implementation for the Entity Framework. You have a fully pluggable DAL for the Domain Model that is not aware of the mapping model, which you designed using the .edmx designer of the Entity Framework.

Mapping the Domain Using NHibernate

The process to map the domain using NHibernate is simpler and should take less time—but remember, everything depends on the type of DDD approach that you are using. In this case, if you're using a domain-first approach, NHibernate lets you auto-generate everything, from the mapping to the final database schema. If you're using the database-first approach, NHibernate will require more effort than Entity Framework to generate the mapping files.

Getting the Tools

First, go to *www.nhforge.com* and download the latest build or the last available General Availability (GA) release. At the time of this writing, version 3 has been released in beta 2, and it's already pretty stable. After you have downloaded the version that you want to use, go to *www.fluentNHibernate.com* and download the latest version of FluentNHibernate so that you can create the mappings using a few lines of code rather than manually writing error-prone XML files.

Create a new solution in Visual Studio and call it **CRM.DAL.NHibernate**. Add these three references: *CRM.DAL* (the abstract DAL layer), *CRM.Domain* (The Domain Model) and *System. ComponentModel.Composition* (for MEF support).

Find the folder where you installed NHibernate; you should see a set of assemblies that are *mandatory* to run this O/RM. To fully install NHibernate, you should have downloaded three different packages: *NHibernate[version].GA*, the core engine: *LINQtoNHibernate[version].GA*, which supplies support for LINQ; and FluentNHibernate, as discussed at the beginning of this section.

You should reference all three packages in your NHibernate concrete DAL. Refer to Figure 4-11 as a reference.

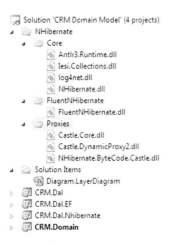

FIGURE 4-11 The required assemblies for NHibernate.

Before we begin, I'll briefly explain this list of assemblies. The folder named Core contains the NHibernate engine; Log4Net.dll, which is an open-source log that's plugged into this O/RM; Iesi.Collection.dll is a proxy collection used by the O/RM; and Antlr3.Runtime.dll is a profiler for the O/RM. FluentNHibernate.dll is self-explanatory. The Proxies folder is one of the available proxy engines for "on-the-fly" creation of proxy classes. You can choose from Castle, LinFu, or Spring; unfortunately, Unity is not available for this O/RM. Select the one you prefer. For demonstration purposes here, I will use Castle, just because it's the simplest to configure.

After referencing all the assemblies, you can begin to build your NHibernate mapping and session factory. Let's start with the *UnitOfWork*. You want to do the same thing you did for the Entity Framework DAL: create a new *UnitOfWork* that inherits from *CRM.DAL.IUnitOfWork* and implement each concrete method.

The *UnitOfWork* and the *ISession*

The *UnitOfWork* for NHibernate is slightly different because there's no *ObjectContext* object. Instead, we have an *ISession* object generated by the Session Factory. Here's how it works:

```
[Export(typeof(IUnitOfWork))]
public class UnitOfWork : IUnitOfWork
{
    private ITransaction tx;

    private ISession orm;

    public UnitOfWork(ISession orm)
    {
        this.orm = orm;
    }
```

The *ISession* interface is more powerful than the *ObjectContext* object provided by Entity Framework, and it's also more flexible. Unfortunately, due to its characteristics you must provide all the necessary code to execute a correct business transaction. The *ISession* itself will keep the transaction alive as long as you want.

```
    public void BeginTransaction()
    {
        if (tx != null)
        {
            tx = orm.BeginTransaction();
        }
    }

    public void CommitTransaction()
    {
        if (tx == null)
        {
            throw new Exception("The current transaction has not been initialized.");
        }
        tx.Commit();
    }

    public void RollbackTransaction()
    {
        if (tx == null)
        {
            throw new Exception("The current transaction has not been initialized.");
        }
        tx.Rollback();
    }
```

The other methods are pretty close to what you've already seen with Entity Framework. The main difference is that NHibernate doesn't need to get attached to an existing entity if you disposed the *ISession*. NHibernate's persistence ignorance mechanism is able to understand whether an entity is a new entity or an existing one.

NHibernate has very specific management for the Domain Session, represented by the Session Factory, a static class that is able to generate all the required proxies and connections for the O/RM in one shot. Your DAL will retrieve the Session from the Session Factory, which will return a new UoW. The sample code uses the FluentNHibernate plug-in, and the short excerpt that follows shows you how to create an automatic mapping (*Domain fields = database fields*) with just one call:

```
[Export(typeof(ISessionFactory))]
public class SessionFactory : ISessionFactory
{
    private IUnitOfWork uow;

    public IUnitOfWork CurrentUoW {
        get
        {
            if (uow == null)
            {
                uow = GetUnitOfWork();
            }

            return uow;
        }
    }

    public SessionFactory()
    {

    }

    /// <summary>
    /// Gets the unit of work.
    /// </summary>
    /// <returns></returns>
    private IUnitOfWork GetUnitOfWork()
    {
        var session = Fluently.Configure()
            .Database(
                MsSqlConfiguration.MsSql2008
                .ConnectionString(x => x.FromAppSetting("DatabaseConnection")))
                .Mappings(m => m.AutoMappings
                    .Add(AutoMap.AssemblyOf<Person>)
                    .Add(AutoMap.AssemblyOf<Customer>)
                    .Add(AutoMap.AssemblyOf<Employee>)
                .BuildConfiguration();
        var uow = new UnitOfWork(session);
        return uow;
    }
```

This sample created a new SQL 2008 session which, like the Entity Framework session, will retrieve the connection string from the App.Config/Web.Config and create an automapping for each entity added to the configuration. That's it. Using a domain-first approach you don't need to do anything else—the *ISession* is ready for use.

The Repository

I left the repository implementation until the end of the tutorial because it should not be different between the two O/RMs. The only difference is that in the Entity Framework, you will query the *ObjectContext* object, while in NHibernate, you will query the *ISession* object.

The only important thing for taking advantage of lazy loading and dynamic SQL creation is to always return an *IQueryable<T>* collection.

The following code uses the Entity Framework *UnitOfWork* to retrieve a list of *Customers*:

```
public IQueryable<T> GetList<T>() where T : class
{
    return ((ObjectContext)this.UoW.orm).CreateObjectSet<T>();
}
```

Here's the same code using the NHibernate Repository:

```
public IQueryable<T> GetList<T>() where T : class
{
    return ((ISession)this.UoW.orm).Linq<T>();
}
```

Both of these repositories allow you to write something such as this:

```
var customers = GetList<Customer>()
    .Where(c => c.FirstName == "John")
    .OrderBy(c => c.FirstName)
```

The implementation will be the same for all the repository implementations. In this way, we will use the *IQueryable<T>* objects without the need to know what DAL we are really using in the MVVM layers.

Summary

In this chapter, you've seen a number of concepts, the O/RM being among them. If you have not yet worked with an O/RM, you should review the sample code for this book and spend some time investigating documentation and tutorials based on the O/RM that you choose. The purpose of the exercise in this chapter is to show you how to write dynamic and recyclable code. Of course, in a real-world MVVM LOB application, you will probably never need to map your Domain Model to two different O/RMs—but the point is that if you follow these techniques, you will be able to recycle parts of your code for your next MVVM application.

You saw that we can still use the "classic style" of writing custom T-SQL code—or you can spend less time and focus more on the business logic of an application by delegating the hard work to an O/RM. An O/RM is nothing more than an application framework used to help translate a Domain Model into something that the database understands, all without losing the powerful POCO concepts of having the Domain unaware of the persistence mechanism.

There are other O/RMs available for the .NET Framework, but the most popular (and free) are the Entity Framework and NHibernate. While the Entity Framework is designed more for a database-first approach, NHibernate is more flexible when used with a domain-first approach. However, you saw that either O/RM can be used with either of these two DDD approaches.

Chapter 5
The Business Layer

After completing this chapter, you will be able to:

- Create and execute Business Rules.

- Create the correct Business Logic Layer.

- Apply the knowledge acquired to the sample application.

Introduction

One of the most time-consuming tasks—and probably the most expensive in terms of maintenance—is the Business Layer of your application (provided, of course, that the application you are working on has one).

In both old-fashioned and modern applications, the Business Layer is generally composed of a nested set of classes. Some applications store the business logic in the Domain Layer; others store it in the database using stored procedures or views. The worst applications store the business logic in a haphazard manner, scattered throughout the code.

There are few things less enjoyable than trying to maintain an application that has business logic strewn all over. Not only will you waste a lot of time just trying to figure out how the code works, but every change you make could cause unexpected behaviors in other sections of the application.

In a clean, modern design, the Business Layer should be a separate layer of your application. It should be aware of the Domain Layer and probably also the Data Layer. The Business Layer is the logical core of any Line of Business (LOB) application, and it should be the only place where the business logic of your application resides. It should also be easy to maintain and self-documenting.

In an Model View ViewModel (MVVM) application, the Business Layer is composed of a set of Services and Business Rules that define the business processes which the program is designed to perform. This layer is exposed and used by the ViewModels that should include only the presentation logic. This scheme lets you maintain a loose coupling between the business logic and the presentation logic.

> **Note** While the term "Business Rules" is often used to mean any non-UI logic, in this book, the term includes only logic that implements business processes and ensures data integrity. This code is independent of the client portion of the application.

Before exploring how to accomplish the goal of keeping the business logic separate from the views and the domain entities in the sample CRM application, I want to explain the difference between validation rules and business rules.

A Business Rule Is Not a Validation Rule

A Validation Rule is any criterion that describes how to validate a specific value of a specific object. Examples include the field length constraint for a database table, or the "Required Field" messages displayed in a View. Validation Rules are usually applied to an object that needs to be validated *before* its value is saved to the data store or *before* it's processed by another transaction that requires the value to be valid.

In contrast, a Business Rule is any rule that acts to *change the value* of an object, based on a set of rules or based on a specific behavior. Often, Business Rules have the sole purpose of informing users whether an action can or cannot be executed after the evaluation of specific objects involved in that transaction.

> **Note** I have noticed that many people do not make a distinction between Business Rules and Validation Rules. Because both serve the same master, you can lump both types of rules together—but you should be aware that there are two different types of rules. The first type ensures data integrity and validity, and belong to what this book calls Validation Rules, the second type handles business processes and operations; in this book, those are called Business Rules.

Usually, you define Validation Rules in two distinct layers: the Domain Model and the UI. In the first case, you set up constraints to ensure a Domain Entity is valid before saving it to a data store or processing it with another component. You can define these rules manually using procedural code, using third-party frameworks, or through simple decoration attributes. The following code shows how you might validate an object using the *System. ComponentModel* namespace available with the Microsoft .NET Framework:

```
/// <summary>
/// Gets or sets the first name.
/// </summary>
/// <value>The first name.</value>
[Required(ErrorMessage = "The First Name can't be null or empty.")]
[StringLength(50, ErrorMessage = "The First Name can't be greater than 50 characters.")]
public string FirstName { get; set; }
```

The preceding code defined some simple validation rules on the *Person* Domain Entity, specifically, on its *FirstName* property. We want to ensure that the property value isn't blank and that it doesn't exceed 50 characters in length. Each validation error is associated with a specific error message. In Chapter 6, "The UI Layer with MVVM," you'll see how you can easily bind these properties to the ViewModel.

A second application of this rule lies in the UI layer. For example, in a simple LOB Silverlight application, you might encounter validation behavior when trying to log on using improper credentials. Figure 5-1 shows a classic validation rule applied to a Silverlight MVVM view.

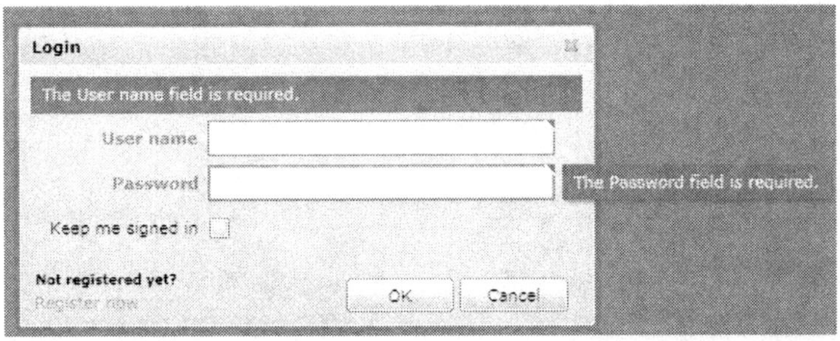

FIGURE 5-1 Silverlight view with a validation message.

A Business Rule uses a different approach because it is composed of a set of rules that aren't easily defined using a simple attribute approach. Typically, you need to write *if/else* statements or *switch* statements, depending on the type of ruleset that you want to verify. The .NET Framework includes a free and useful tool to accomplish this task: Windows Workflow Foundation version 4 (WF 4.0). Of course, the problem here is not only about writing complex *if/else* or *switch* statements. It's about the application logic you use to implement a business process or to ensure that a complex set of rules is applied, which you can't express as a single attribute on a property.

For example, you can consider the workflow shown in Figure 5-2 as a set of rules.

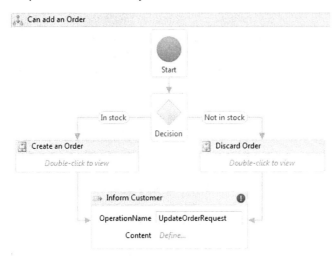

FIGURE 5-2 A custom workflow to create an order.

The workflow in Figure 5-2 executes a set of Business Rules to verify that a submitted *Order* can be fulfilled; for example, whether a requested product is in stock and available to be shipped. If verification succeeds, then the *Order* will be created, and a message will be sent to the queue. Otherwise, the order will be discarded, and a different message will be sent to the queue to inform the customer that the product is not in stock.

You can also accomplish this process by using the following pseudo C# code:

```csharp
public class CustomRules
{
    [Import]
    private IRepository repository;
    public void CanAddAnOrder(Order order, Customer customer)
    {
        foreach (var orderLine in order.OrderLines)
        {
            var available =
                repository.GetEntity<Product>(orderLine.Product.PrimaryKey)
                .AmountInStock;
            if (!available)
            {
                RemoveOrder(order, customer);
                break;
            }
        }
```

```
                ConfirmOrder(order, customer);
        }
    }


        private void RemoveOrder(Order order, Customer customer) { }
        private void ConfirmOrder(Order order, Customer customer) { }
    }
```

This second example demonstrates that translating the ruleset to a programming language is a potentially error-prone process. More than that, this ruleset is totally incomprehensible to anyone not fluent in code, such as an analyst or an account manager, who also need to know how this ruleset works. In addition, the process of maintaining up-to-date documentation for such rules can be time-consuming.

In contrast, when you use a graphical tool such as WF 4.0 to implement a ruleset, you can share the rules with programmers involved in the development process and non-coders, alike. In other words, the visual representation makes your rule code more readable and maintainable to all participants.

In this chapter, you'll see other third-party tools available for using this "workflow-by-design" approach, and why that approach is much better than having custom C# code spread throughout the layers of your LOB applications. First, consider the testability of your Business Rules; if they are part of a specific layer/component, you can test them easily against a set of mockup data. Second, consider the documentation: a visual workflow is also readable and understandable by non-technical persons such as an operations employee, or an auditor who might need to verify the business logic applied to the application.

Business Rules by Service

Business Rules need to be stored inside a layer, and probably the best place to do that is in an additional assembly visible to the Business Layer. That is not an additional layer but an extension of the Business Logic Layer (BLL) that includes only the physical workflows. It doesn't matter nearly as much which technology you use to create your business rules (whether workflows, procedural code, or XML files), but it's important that you keep these rules separate from any other code in your LOB application so that you can easily separate maintenance and test processes.

It's also useful to execute these rules with code that uses the same format throughout your LOB application so that you can easily recognize a call to a Business Rule and apply them in a consistent way.

The Design by Service is a design pattern introduced by Martin Fowler, in which the core of your business transaction runs in a service that knows everything about the Model and the Data Layer. It is also the only object in charge of making business decisions.

By using Design by Service in the Business Layer, you delegate the execution of a rule or set of rules, object validation, and specific business transactions to a service class that doesn't need anything more than the objects involved in the process. The best way to do that is to create a set of service classes based on the business transactions that your application will execute. The more granular the codes in this part of the application, the easier it will be to maintain this important layer.

Pseudo code for such a service class would look similar to this:

```
var svc = Container.Resolve<IService<Customer>>();
var order = svc.CreateProcess(ProcessEnum.CreateOrder, myPerson, myOrderLines);
var result = svc.Verify(RulesEnum.AddOrder, myPerson, order);
```

The preceding code is a simple generic class that can execute workflows based on the type of operation that you want to perform. The class is flexible, readable, and easy to maintain. You can define the operations using a set of enumeration values to add more readability to the code, and then refer to a specific workflow with the same name.

The Facade Pattern

Another interesting way would be to use one or more of the design patterns we saw in Chapter 2, "The Design Patterns," to make the Business Layer more flexible. For example, the Facade pattern would be a good match for the base service that exposes simple methods through a common facade interface, which hides the real interaction between the systems. In the following example, we want to expose an *AddOrder* method within our facade, but we don't want to require developers to know what is going on behind that process.

Figure 5-3 illustrates a classic Facade service layer. Each facade in this case uses generic implementation to identify the primary entity involved in the process, and each service exposes some business methods that execute a set of transactions that are not visible outside the facade service. For example, the method *CanAddOrder* executes additional methods inside its signature, such as:

- *IsProductAvailable*
- *IsOrderCompleted*
- *CanCustomerSubmitOrder*

Because these three additional methods are marked as private, they are not visible outside the Facade service. This way, you can keep the code separate, but also make using the service layer less error-prone, because it forces developers to call only the exposed methods, such as *CanAddOrder* and doesn't provide direct access to the shortcut methods used by the facade.

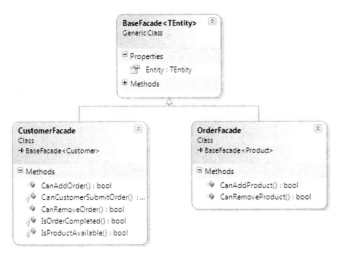

FIGURE 5-3 A business service using the Facade pattern.

Business Rules by Workflow with WF 4.0

When you build your Business Layer, it's important that you provide a means for non-technical but business-savvy people to read and understand it—just like the Domain Model. Using the right combination of Domain Model and Business Layer, a non-programmer should be able to understand the design of your application and the business logic behind the application.

In the previous section, you learned that it's difficult to embed custom generic logic in a C# procedure and make it self-documenting. Of course, you can write a nice, clean fluent interface, but often that's not enough, especially because the Business Layer often continues to grow and change throughout an application's lifetime.

WF 4.0, which ships with the .NET Framework 4, has an updated workflow engine built around XAML code—just like a normal MVVM application. This version is completely different from the previous version; it's both very flexible and allows you to build custom workflows and rulesets for your Business Layer.

The basic concept of WF 4.0 is to simplify writing a procedural workflow that can make decisions and adapt, based on values it receives as input parameters. Of course, these values can be either from one or more domain model entities, or just simple scalar values.

The following example uses a new "Workflow Activity Library" project type, available with .NET Framework 4 and Microsoft Visual Studio 2010. I have added two references to the project: one to the generic Data Layer that you created in Chapter 4, "The Data Layer," and one to the Domain Model that you created in Chapter 3, "The Domain Model." This workflow is intended to ensure that a user can add and confirm an *Order*. In this case, there will be two parameters: the current *Customer* and the *Order* to process.

To begin, the workflow includes one *if* statement to verify that the products in the *Order* are available. Each product has an *AmountInStock* property that tells us how many items are in stock. Each *OrderLine* of a product has a *Quantity* property and a *Product* property. The rule basically applies this concept: *If the amount requested is greater than the availability in stock the Order can't be processed.* Figure 5-4 documents this process by using WF 4.0.

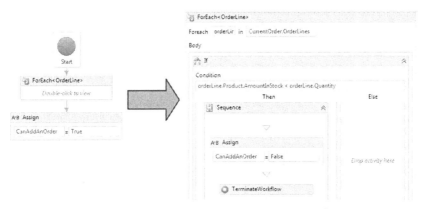

FIGURE 5-4 The workflow for the Add Order Business Transaction.

In this example, you are passing two input parameters to the workflow: *CurrentCustomer* and *CurrentOrder*. You retrieve a *Boolean* output parameter called *CanAddOrder*. Calling this from the final code will look something like this:

```
var customer = MVVMView.CurrentCustomer;
var order = MVVMView.CurrentOrder;
var canAddOrder = OrderService.CanAddOrder(customer, order);
if (canAddOrder)
{
    customer.AddOrder(order);
    uow.Save(customer);
}
```

Of course, you should also start and close a transaction—this code assumes that the *Order* and the *Customer* have been validated prior to the code beginning.

Different Ways of Running a Workflow

WF 4.0 offers two ways to run a workflow. A workflow by itself is nothing more than an XAML file compiled inside a .dll project (an Activities Library). .NET 4 can read these special XAML files, deserialize them on the fly, and then pass them to the WF engine executor, or it can process an XAML file embedded in a class library by using the Workflow Application object.

WorkFlowInvoker

The first (and simplest) method to run a workflow (which was inherited from version 3 of the Workflow engine) is called *WorkflowInvoker*. This class requires that the workflow you want to run is already in hand, so you must either know the real code file name of the workflow or have the XAML code. It works in the following way:

```
// first of all you render the workflow in memory
Activity wf;
using (Stream xaml = File.OpenRead("CanAddOrder.xaml"))
{
    wf = ActivityXamlServices.Load(xaml);
}
```

Next, you call the static Workflow Engine and pass it any input and output parameters inside an *IDictionary<string, object>* collection, where the key of the collection is the parameter name, and the object is the current value.

```
var params = new Dictionary<string, object>
{
    { "CurrentCustomer", myCustomer },
    { "CurrentOrder", myOrder },
}
// execute the workflow
var output = WorkflowInvoker.Invoke(wf, params);
// access the result
Console.Writeline("Can Execute? {0}", output["CanExecute"]);
```

The *WorkflowInvoker* returns another collection of type *<string, object>*, which includes all the available output parameters.

Pros and Cons of the *WorkflowInvoker*

The *WorkflowInvoker* is fairly simple and easy to use. In fact, it's *too* simple; it doesn't give you much control over the workflow. For example, you can't track the status of the workflow, and you can't monitor the execution by using events. Therefore, you should use *WorkflowInvoker* only for simple workflows such as *CanExecute* on a Context Menu or a Button command. You might also use it for testing your workflows before going into production, but keep in mind that *WorkflowInvoker* is not designed for a more complex environment.

WorkflowApplication and WCF

If you plan to build your MVVM application's BLL using WF 4.0, you should concentrate on the more complex hosting engine, called *WorkflowApplication*. This component uses the same collections of input and output parameters, but you also have access to specific events and asynchronous calls by which you can build a more complex and sophisticated rule engine.

To run a workflow this way, you first need to retrieve your current workflow. To do that, you don't need to know the XAML path, just the class name available in the DLL, as shown in the following example:

```
WorkflowApplication wf = new WorkflowApplication(new CanAddOrder());
// parameters
var params = new Dictionary<string, object>
{
    { "CurrentCustomer", myCustomer },
    { "CurrentOrder", myOrder },
}
```

Then you create a new instance of the non-static *WorkflowApplication* and subscribe to all the available events, so that you can have full control over the execution of the ruleset:

```
wf.Completed = delegate(WorkflowApplicationCompletedEventArgs e)
{
    // Handle the execution Complete
};
wf.Aborted = delegate(WorkflowApplicationAbortedEventArgs e)
{
    // handle the execution aborted
};
wf.OnUnhandledException =
  delegate(WorkflowApplicationUnhandledExceptionEventArgs e)
{
    // handle the failure
        return UnhandledExceptionAction.Terminate;
};
wf.Run();
```

Using this approach, you can execute the ruleset on a middle tier, for example, which might be faster and more powerful than the client's PC, or you can simply monitor the execution of a workflow and make business decisions without throwing exceptions in UI.

AppFabric and the WCF Execution

Microsoft AppFabric is a set of integrated technologies that make it easier to build, scale, and manage web and composite applications that run on IIS and Windows Server. Windows Server AppFabric is available at *http://msdn.microsoft.com/en-us/windowsserver/ee695849*. You can download and install it through the easy-to-use web platform Installer component.

One feature of AppFabric is that it provides the possibility to host and execute Windows Workflows through a set of WCF Services, so that the BLL of your application can be stored in a separate application server. Because AppFabric is also based on .NET Framework 4, it provides—out of the box—a set of persistence, monitoring, and hosting functionalities that can be useful when you are building an application server that needs to host one or more application BLLs.

AppFabric is a complex product that probably deserves an entire book, but the point here is that AppFabric is absolutely the answer for building a medium to complex BLL with a scalable and maintainable application server. To support this claim and to help you understand the product better, here is a list of features that Windows AppFabric server makes available:

- Deployment and management of WCF and WF Services hosted using WAS
- Configuration and persistence of workflows, their statuses, and their execution results
- Dedicated queryable storage for management
- Full integration with Windows PowerShell
- Customizable monitoring of hosted services

Pros and Cons of *WorkflowApplication*

If you plan to use the *WorkflowApplication* engine, the considerations are essentially the opposite of those for using the *WorkflowInvoker*. The *WorkflowApplication* class requires more effort, but it allows you to write a more stable and powerful workflow executor. At the same time, it provides more control and options that you might need if you plan to use WF as your unique ruleset engine.

WF also offers many additional features, such as hosting a workflow directly in your WPF application, or persisting the status of a workflow in SQL, so you can pause and restore the workflow execution as required.

For this and other features, see the WF documentation and other information available at *http://msdn.microsoft.com/en-us/netframework/aa663328.aspx*.

Third-Party Toolkits

In this case, the Business Layer will be very complex and you will probably not have the time to learn and master a complex technology such as WF. You must also keep in mind that WF is an open technology, so to customize it to satisfy your customer's needs, you will need to spend some time on it.

I have also noticed that usually, in a big environment, the Business Layer is incorrectly left to the analyst side, where they know how to write the business rules, but unfortunately, most of the time, they don't know how to translate these rules into something usable by an MVVM application. In such cases, you should consider using a third-party tool which will alleviate the effort involved; you will just need to plug this technology into your BLL. There are usually suitable third-party tools that can provide analysts with an easy-to-use workflow designer and at the same time extend a powerful rule engine to developers that can be plugged into any LOB application.

Technologies for the Data Validation

The Microsoft Enterprise Library, currently at version 5.0, will probably satisfy all your requirements for adding data validation to your Domain Entities. You can obtain Enterprise Library here at *http://msdn.microsoft.com/en-us/library/ff632023.aspx*. Enterprise Library ships with a Validation Application Block (VAB); a useful framework that provides a default set of validation rules, plus a powerful and customizable rule engine.

> **Note** Remember that data validation should be enforced not only on the Domain Model but also in the ViewModel of your MVVM UI, and in any place where data validation is required by design.

Basically, VAB lets you decorate classes with the validation rules provided by the Library or with custom rules that you provide. Later, you can validate the object and retrieve any validation errors. The following code illustrates how to perform basic validation using the VAB library:

```
using Microsoft.Practices.EnterpriseLibrary.Validation;
using Microsoft.Practices.EnterpriseLibrary.Validation.Validators;
public class Customer
{
  [StringLengthValidator(0, 20)]
  public string CustomerName;

  public Customer(string customerName)
  {
    this.CustomerName = customerName;
  }
}
public class MyExample
{
  private ValidatorFactory factory;
  public MyExample(ValidatorFactory valFactory)
  {
    factory = valFactory;
  }
```

```
public void MyMethod()
{
   Customer myCustomer = new Customer("A name that is too long");
   Validator<Customer> customerValidator
                    = factory.CreateValidator<Customer>();
   // Validate the instance to obtain a collection of validation errors.
   ValidationResults r = customerValidator.Validate(myCustomer);
   if (!r.IsValid)
   {
      throw new InvalidOperationException("Validation error found.");
   }
}
}
```

VAB contains a default set of validation attributes that include the following:

- Contains Characters Validator
- Date Time Range Validator
- Domain Validator
- Enum Conversion Validator
- Not Null Validator
- Object Collection Validator
- Object Validator
- Or Composite Validator
- Property Comparison Validator
- Range Validator
- Regular Expression Validator
- Relative Date Time Validator
- String Length Validator
- Type Conversion Validator
- Single Member Validators

You might also be interested in other third-party validation frameworks; most of these are both reliable and open source, meaning that you don't need to purchase licenses to use them in your MVVM application. Additional validation frameworks that you want to explore for .NET are:

- EVIL (*http://evil.codeplex.com*)   An open-source project that works much like the VAB library, using decorations and rulesets.

- Active Record (*http://www.castleproject.org/activerecord/index.html*)   An open-source plug-in for NHibernate that transforms your domain into an Active Record domain.

- Conditions (*http://conditions.codeplex.com*)   Another open-source framework that uses the Fluent Interface (see Chapter 2) instead of attributes.

Rule Engine and Business Rule Engine

When you move to the concepts of Business Rules, the argument becomes more complex. A Business Rule engine should usually be able to execute custom rules, provide a fluent syntax that is understandable by non-technical users, and provide an easy-to-read and modifiable authoring tool.

Of course, if you are looking for all these requirements in one tool, ready to use, you will probably need to test and purchase a third-party Business Rule engine—which won't be free.

The two tools you'll see here are the most popular for .NET. That doesn't necessarily mean that they are the best or the most flexible tools available for all purposes. In addition, these tools have a starting price close to 100,000 USD.

There are various tools available online; the one shown here and the next one are just some of them, and in no way does it mean that you should adopt this particular tool as your business rule engine.

InRule for .NET

InRule is a very flexible and easy to use Business Rules engine that you can easily plug into any .NET application. It provides user controls for editing rules directly within your application, and it has a straightforward, easy to understand infrastructure.

InRule might not be the most scalable solution, but the price is nowhere near as high as many other Business Rules engines. You can download a demonstration version of InRule from *http://www.inrule.com* and run the available tutorials to see how to use the tool.

Figure 5-5 shows a custom Silverlight application using InRule to edit some Business Rules.

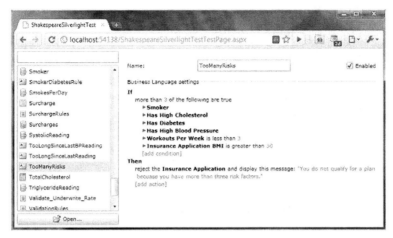

FIGURE 5-5 The InRule Silverlight authoring tool.

Business Layer Considerations

In this chapter, you've seen how complex a Business Layer can be and why it's a requirement for your MVVM applications. Of course, having a Business Layer in your application can introduce some problems that you need to consider.

When Do I Need to Create a Business Layer?

It's a good practice to always try to understand whether a feature is truly needed in your MVVM application so that you can avoid over-engineering. The Business Layer can be less or more complicated, and you should always keep in mind the following notes before starting to create a BLL in your application:

- If you need to execute a significant number of operations and/or business rules to persist new data in your application's data store, it's probably a good idea to create a BLL layer in your application. On the other hand, if you only need to save and retrieve data from a database and display it a UI, designing and using a BLL is probably overkill.

- If you need to validate your objects before saving them in your datastore or before moving to the next step of your application flow, a BLL is a good way to keep the validation process isolated from the rest of the application. However, when you are working with basic data that doesn't need much or any validation, you don't need a BLL.

- If the logic of your application is dynamic, complex, and incremental (meaning that it will grow and change during the development process) and needs to be documented for auditing purposes, you *must* have a BLL—and you will probably also need to consider purchasing a Business Rules engine. By doing this, you will also be able to keep your BLL separated from the other application components and allow it to evolve independently.

To sum up, if your application requires any significant amount of business logic and/or data validation, you should consider creating a BLL to keep that functionality separate from the rest of your application code. That will simplify both application maintenance and help with documentation.

Bad BLL Habits

The last few words regarding BLLs are about bad habits I've encountered that you should always avoid.

First, the BLL is not the Unit of Work (UoW) of your application, and it is not the Repository for your Data Access Layer. The BLL has atomic methods that can execute a set of business transactions, such as:

```
var result = BLL.CanAddOrderToCustomer(myCustomer, myOrder);
```

It's very likely that the *CanAddOrderToCustomer* method implements a set of operations that involve the UoW, the Repository, and the Domain Model, such as in the following example:

```
public void CanAddOrderToCustomer(myCustomer, myOrder)
{
    UnitOfWork.StartTransaction();
    var available =  repository.Get<Order>(myOrder).AmountInStock;
    if (available)
    {
        myCustomer.Orders.Create(myOrder);

        repository.Update<Customer>(myCustomer);
        ... ...
    }
}
```

This doesn't mean that a BLL should have a method like *GetCustomer(int id)*, because this method should be exposed by the Repository, not implemented in the BLL. More than likely, there will be another place in the application that doesn't need to use BLL functionality but needs to load a customer by ID.

Second, the BLL is the layer that you use to speak "business language," so you should always use a clear and neat naming convention. A method that verifies whether an order can be added should be called something like *CanCustomerCreateOrder* or *CanItemBePurchased* instead of the shorter but less understandable *AddOrder* or *PurchaseItem*. Remember that the BLL includes the business logic of the application, so you will eventually need to change or upgrade it, either because the business logic has been revised or the process has changed.

Finally, test, test, and test again. You must test each method of the BLL with real data, especially if the BLL executes calculations and statistics. Every single method must be examined with a set of fully reliable tests that you can run in the future, when you have to update the application's business logic.

Sample Code: The Business Service Layer

Now that we have the Domain Model in place, and we know how to persist and retrieve the Domain Model from the database, we need a smart way to execute business logic rules against the Domain Model and to validate the Domain Entities using a specific set of Validation Rules.

For the validation process, the example CRM application will use the Enterprise Library 5.0; specifically, this example makes use of the VAB and C# generics to build a generic validator.

For Business Rules, the application uses Windows WF 4.0. You'll also see how to create a simple *FluentEngine* that is able to run any workflow you want.

Data Validation with the Enterprise Library 5.0

The first step is to download the latest version of the Enterprise Library, which is available at *http://entlib.codeplex.com*. Then you need to run the *Build* command available in the Enterprise Library 5.0 setup. You should now have two folders (depending on the setup options you chose): one containing the Enterprise Library source code, and one with a compiled deployed version. The DLL that you need is named Microsoft.Practices. EnterpriseLibrary.Validation.dll.

Add a reference to this DLL in the CRM.Domain layer so that you can add Data Validation rules for each Domain entity. The following code example shows the *Person* entity with some basic data validation rules applied:

```
/// <summary>
/// Gets or sets the first name.
/// </summary>
/// <value>The first name.</value>
[NotNullValidator(ErrorMessage = "The First Name can't be null or empty.")]
[StringLengthValidator(50, ErrorMessage =
    "The First Name lenght can't be greater than 50 characters.")]
public string FirstName { get; set; }

/// <summary>
/// Gets or sets the last name.
/// </summary>
/// <value>The last name.</value>
```

```
[NotNullValidator(ErrorMessage = "The Last Name can't be null or empty.")]
[StringLengthValidator(50, ErrorMessage =
    "The Last Name lenght can't be greater than 50 characters.")]
public string LastName { get; set; }

/// <summary>
/// Gets or sets the birth date.
/// </summary>
/// <value>The birth date.</value>
[NotNullValidator(ErrorMessage = "The Birth Date can't be null or empty.")]
[RelativeDateTimeValidator(18, DateTimeUnit.Year,100,DateTimeUnit.Year,
    ErrorMessage = "The Birth Date can't be lower than 18 years.")]
public DateTime BirthDate { get; set; }
```

The preceding code tries to reflect the database schema constraints in the Domain Entities so that the application can validate each entity before saving or retrieving it from the database. You can then apply this step in the UoW so that every entity passed to it can be self-validated before committing the transaction.

Now we need to validate this entity, and if it's not valid, we should return a *Boolean* result in conjunction with a collection of errors generated by the validation process. Every entity that is inherited from a Domain Base Object can be validated, so there is no better place than the Domain Object to introduce this validation process. By design, the VAB exposes a collection called *ValidationResults* that contains the results of a validation process and a *Boolean* property called *IsValid*. You can retrieve the validation collection by using the *Validator* class exposed by the application block.

First, let's open the Domain Object class and add a read-only property that exposes the validation results:

```
/// <summary>
/// Gets the validation errors.
/// </summary>
/// <value>The errors.</value>
public ValidationResults Errors { get; private set; }
```

Now, we need to expose an *IsValid* property, which will fire the validation process behind the scenes. Before doing that, I want to show you how you apply the Validation Facade pattern to the VAB. When you want to validate a new object, you can simply use the Validation Factory facade provided in the library. Unfortunately, the syntax of the Facade is as follows:

```
// option using generics
var validator = ValidationFactory.CreateValidator<T>();
// second option without generics
var validator = ValidationFactory.CreateValidator(Type);
```

This means that you cannot expose the method from the base class without exposing its generic signature; otherwise, when you call this method from an inherited class, the validation will validate only the base class properties. A smart solution might be:

```
/// <summary>
/// Gets or sets a value indicating whether this instance is valid.
/// </summary>
/// <value><c>true</c> if this instance is valid; otherwise, <c>false</c>.</value>
public virtual bool IsValid { get; private set; }

/// <summary>
/// Validates this instance.
/// </summary>
/// <typeparam name="T"></typeparam>
/// <returns></returns>
protected bool Validate<T>()
{
    Errors = ValidationFactory.CreateValidator<T>().Validate(this);
    return Errors.IsValid;
}
```

Now you can override the validation process if you want (note that the preceding change marked the property as *virtual*, and not *abstract*). When you need to implement a validation process, such as in the *Person* class we previously decorated with the Enterprise Library attributes, you can simply override the *IsValid* property in this way:

```
/// <summary>
/// Gets or sets a value indicating whether this instance is valid.
/// </summary>
/// <value><c>true</c> if this instance is valid; otherwise, <c>false</c>.</value>
public override bool IsValid
{
    get
    {
        return base.Validate<Person>();
    }
}
```

At this point, you have a simple validator that you can recycle throughout the Domain Model. Using the same Facade pattern, you can validate the ViewModel in the same way.

For more in-depth information about Enterprise Library, download the complete documentation in PDF form from the CodePlex website at *http://entlib.codeplex.com/releases/view/46741*. The documentation includes a wealth of samples and tutorials.

A Generic Workflow Engine

Earlier, this chapter showed how Workflow Foundation can be the perfect solution for building an in-house Business Rules engine. While the syntax to load and run a workflow is not ideal, by using the Fluent Language pattern that was presented in Chapter 2, you can create a fluent engine that's both easy to use and able to process any workflow.

Remember, you have two options for running a workflow: the skinny, static *WorkflowInvoker*, or the more complex *WorkflowApplication*. Using the second option, you can monitor the status of a workflow and add custom runtime behaviors (such as writing to a specific log) or attach events.

Let's start by adding the infrastructure to create the fluent syntax. The schema in Figure 5-6 shows the UML diagram for a Fluent Workflow Engine. Using this engine, you can load an assembly that contains a set of Workflows, load a specific Workflow, create listeners for WF events using lambda syntax, and of course, run the workflow.

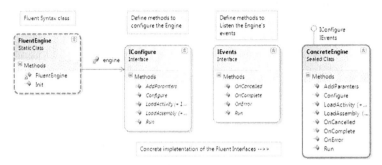

FIGURE 5-6 The UML Schema for the Fluent Engine.

Note If you don't remember how to build a fluent Interface, review the "DSL: Writing Fluent Code" section on page 53, in Chapter 2.

Here, I have created two interfaces so that the fluent interface will have two major steps. The first step loads and initializes a workflow. In the second step, you configure the events to which you want to listen. Both interfaces can directly run the workflow—but if you don't at least listen for the *onComplete* event, you won't know when workflow execution completes.

The static class is used only to create a more fashionable fluent syntax to avoid the ugly use of the *new* keyword.

The final syntax used to run a workflow should look something like the following:

```
//Init the engine class
FluentEngine.Init()
    //load assembly and workflow
    .LoadAssembly("MyWorkflowLibrary.dll")
    .LoadActivity("CanAddAnOrder.xaml")
    //prepare the parameters collection
    // it should contains input/output params
    .AddParamters(new Dictionary<string, object>
```

```
{
    { "Order", null },
    { "Customer", null }
})
.Configure()
//when the WF is done
.OnComplete(() => {
    Console.WriteLine("Complete!");
})
//when the WF raises an error
.OnError((ex) => {
    Console.WriteLine("Error: {0}", ex);
})
.Run();
```

You can use this easy-to-read syntax in the MVVM application to run and monitor a work-flow. For more in-depth information about the workflow engine, the project CRM.BL.WF contains the Workflow Engine implementation and all the workflows for the CRM application example.

Service for Business Transactions

With the base code in place, we need to implement the Facade pattern for the BLL to pre-pare the services for use. In this section, you'll see how to implement the process of adding a New Order service from beginning to end. You can then optionally create custom Business Rules or you can simply open the final project and see how I implemented the BLL.

The first important concept is the user story that will drive this Business Transaction:

> As a User, I want to be able to create an Order and submit the Order by adding the Order to the corresponding Customer, and then send an e-mail confirmation. For each Product in the Order, I need to verify that the Product is in stock.

Figure 5-7 shows the workflow result of this user story, divided into three sections to make it easier to read.

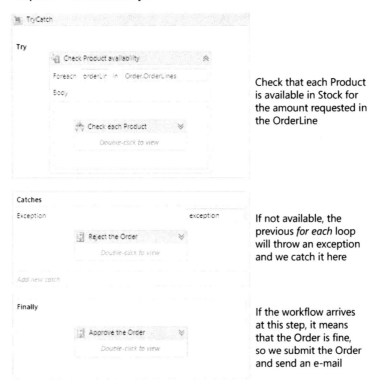

Check that each Product
is available in Stock for
the amount requested in
the OrderLine

If not available, the
previous *for each* loop
will throw an exception
and we catch it here

If the workflow arrives
at this step, it means
that the Order is fine,
so we submit the Order
and send an e-mail

FIGURE 5-7 The complete workflow to add an order.

This workflow requires two input parameters, a *Customer* and an *Order*. It returns a *Boolean*
result. The code to run this workflow should look something like this:

```
public bool CanAddAnOrder(Customer customer, Order order)
{

    //Init the engine class
    FluentEngine.Init()
        //load assembly and workflow
        .LoadAssembly("CRM.BL.WF.dll")
        .LoadActivity("CanAddAnOrder.xaml")
        //prepare the parameters collection
        // it should contains input/output params
        .AddParameters(new Dictionary<string, object>
        {
            { "Order", order },
            { "Customer", customer },
            { "CanAddOrder", false}
        })
        .Configure()
        //when the WF is done
        .OnComplete((parm) => {
            return (bool)parm["CanAddOrder"];
        })
```

```
            //when the WF raises an error
            .OnError((ex) => {
                return false;
            })
            .Run();
    }
```

This workflow also satisfies the compliance office requirements for documenting the code involved in a business transaction.

The previous code should be included in a Facade service. The one used here has *IUnitOfWork* and the main entity involved in the transactions injected at runtime.

In the Business Layer, I have created a basic service that loads the correct *IUnitOfWork* using Managed Extensibility Framework (MEF) (see Chapter 4) at runtime and the corresponding entity using generics. Figure 5-8 shows the basic UML structure of the CRM.BL Layer.

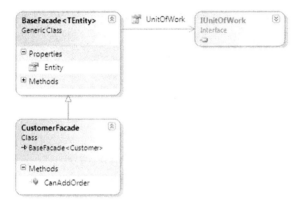

FIGURE 5-8 Structure of a Facade Business Service class.

The code for the base class is pretty straightforward. You have a generic class that requires the current entity as a parameter, which must be of type *DomainObject*, and an *IUnitOfWork* injected at runtime by the MEF engine.

```
public class BaseFacade<TEntity> where TEntity : DomainObject
{
    /// <summary>
    /// Gets or sets the unit of work.
    /// </summary>
    /// <value>The unit of work.</value>
    [Import]
    public IUnitOfWork UnitOfWork { get; private set; }

    /// <summary>
    /// Gets or sets the entity.
    /// </summary>
    /// <value>The entity.</value>
    public TEntity Entity { get; private set; }
```

```
/// <summary>
/// Initializes a new instance of the <see cref="BaseFacade&lt;TEntity&gt;"/> class.
/// </summary>
/// <param name="entity">The entity.</param>
public BaseFacade(TEntity entity)
{
    this.Entity = entity;
}
}
```

From this generic service base class, you can create a specific service class for each entity
and use the UoW or the referenced entity directly within the service. The following code, for
example, is a Facade service for a *Customer* entity. It has a method called *CanAddAnOrder*
that requires only the *Order* entity because the *Customer* entity is injected in the constructor.
MEF creates the *IUnitOfWork* .

Using this solution, you can easily implement the Transaction pattern, where for a series of
business steps, you include everything in a business transaction, implemented in this case by
the UoW and the *Try/Catch* statement.

```
public class CustomerFacade : BaseFacade<Customer>
{
    public CustomerFacade(Customer customer) : base(customer)
    {

    }

    public bool CanAddOrder(Order order)
    {
        try
        {
            bool result = false;
            UnitOfWork.BeginTransaction();

            //previous code to execute the workflow
            // result = EXECUTE WORKFLOW

            if (result)
            {
                Entity.AddOrder(order);
                UnitOfWork.Update(Entity);
            }
            UnitOfWork.CommitTransaction();
            return result;
        }
        catch (Exception ex)
        {
            UnitOfWork.RollbackTransaction();
            throw new ApplicationException(
                "The CanAddOrder process has thrown an exception.", ex);
        }
    }
}
```

This example forms the starting point for any Business Service. By following this approach, you will end up with two layers; one (CRM.BL in the sample code) will be the base layer, which contains all the Facade service classes, the other will be the Workflow Layer (CRM.BL.WF in the sample code), which contains all the Business Rules (Workflows or procedural C# code).

I realize that there's a large effort involved in placing this logic outside the Domain or the Data Layer, but the advantage of this approach becomes clear as soon as you need to change something in the application.

Remember also that if you keep the business logic outside the UI and outside the Domain, you might be able to recycle it for other applications, without the need to rewrite any code.

Summary

The Business Layer, also known as the Business Logic Layer, is probably the most complex and articulated layer of a LOB application. The Business Logic Layer is usually divided into two major parts: Validation Rules and Business Rules. This concept is often misunderstood by developers, but the parts have two radically different purposes.

Validation Rules are in charge of validating the values of an object against a set of basic rules, such as regular expressions, not nullable, string length, and so on. Business Rules are composed of rulesets, which define how an object should behave based on a set of circumstances or values.

You can establish Validation Rules easily using the .NET Framework's *System.ComponentModel* namespace or by using any open source validation library, such as the VAB from the Enterprise Library 5.0.

To implement Business Rules, you can use one of the full-featured (but expensive) third-party frameworks, or you can customize the powerful ruleset engine provided with Windows Workflow Foundation 4.0, as shown in this chapter.

Although building the flexible architecture for the Business Layer is time-consuming, the time you spend building the layer is time that you will save in the future, during application maintenance.

Chapter 6
The UI Layer with MVVM

After completing this chapter, you will be able to:

- Identify the parts that compose the MVVM pattern.
- Apply the command pattern and the WeakEvent manager.
- Provide additional services and facilities for MVVM.

In this chapter, you will finally delve into the Model View ViewModel (MVVM) pattern, and see how it should be implemented to maintain total separation between the XAML-based UI declarative syntax and the UI presentation logic code.

As I mentioned in Chapter 1, "Introduction to Model View ViewModel and Line of Business Applications," Microsoft introduced the MVVM pattern a few years ago, and it's still a hot topic of discussion in many user groups and forums. This chapter includes more than just my personal point of view about how you should implement MVVM to fulfill the basic rules that constitute this pattern.

You want to implement the MVVM pattern in any Line of Business (LOB) application built using Silverlight or Windows Presentation Foundation (WPF) because:

- The whole client application should be fully testable, and to do that, the presentation logic of the View should be separated from the declarative XAML code that composes it. Using a presentation pattern such as MVVM puts more of the application's behavior into non-UI classes that can be tested more easily.
- You want to make the UI designer's job easier by leaving development of the presentation logic to a different team/developer.
- Decoupling the UI logic from the UI declarative markup makes it easy to recycle the ViewModel (the model of the view) for different views.
- You can more easily evolve or change the UI without changing the underlying presentation logic of the application using the power of the *DataTemplate* and *DataBinding* engines provided by XAML markup.

Due to its complex structure, a correct implementation of the MVVM pattern requires a deep understanding of how the *DataTemplate*, *DataBinding*, *Styling*, and *Dependencies* mechanisms work in WPF and Silverlight. However, the purpose of this book is to give you the guidelines for implementing a LOB application using the MVVM pattern—explaining how these mechanisms work on WPF or Silverlight is beyond the scope of this book. I will provide an *overview* of how to use *DataTemplate* and *Commanding*, for example, but if you don't know these concepts in depth, especially *DataTemplate* and *DataBinding*, I suggest that you buy a book specifically about the technology you are planning to use (WPF or Silverlight), and then study and experiment with these two complex XAML mechanisms before starting to struggle with the correct implementation of MVVM itself.

Introduction to the MVVM Pattern

Before starting to implement the MVVM pattern, we should see how it works and what its principal components are.

If you think about a normal layered application, you will notice that the UI is composed of four major objects that constitute the lifecycle of a view (see Figure 6-1): the View, which is a graphical object; a Model, which binds to the view and represents business concepts or entities; a set of controls used for interactions between the View and the user, and that display data from the Model using a binding mechanism; and a set of events raised either by the Model or by the user through the View.

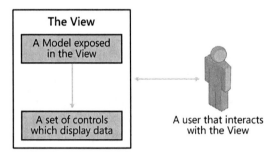

FIGURE 6-1 The general structure of a UI View.

To translate this concept into MVVM, you can say that the View is the XAML UserControl/ Page/Window, which contains a set of controls and the *DataBinding* engine. The Model is one or more Domain Entities exposed by the ViewModel. The ViewModel encapsulates presentation logic in a way that's not specific to the UI, while the View encapsulates the UI itself. You can unit test the ViewModel without the need to resort to complex UI test harnesses, because it is "just code."

Figure 6-2 shows a graphical representation of this concept, using a simple WPF view.

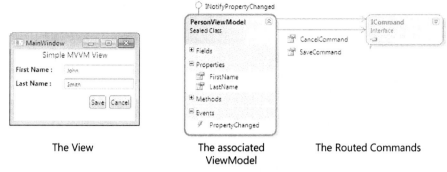

The View   The associated   The Routed Commands
                  ViewModel

FIGURE 6-2 A simple WPF View with an associated ViewModel.

When you bind the ViewModel to the View, you make the ViewModel's properties and events available to the UI so it can provide a user interface for them. Interactions between the View and the ViewModel occur through data bindings, commands, and so on.

At this point, the challenge is to know how to customize the *DataTemplate* of the View to bind these properties correctly, and of course, which properties to expose in the ViewModel. Data templates are a specific way of defining the UI without code-behind—essentially a way to define a View so that it is bound to a ViewModel automatically. Data templates are a way to construct the UI, but they are not the main challenge.

The View

In the MVVM pattern, the View is the graphical interface in charge of displaying data to users and interacting with them. If you're writing a WPF application, the View might be a *UserControl*, a *Window*, or a *Page*; however, in a Silverlight application, the View will be a Silverlight User Control or a Silverlight Page or a Silverlight Child Window (a pop-up).

To make the View MVVM compatible, you first need to add a reference to the corresponding ViewModel in the *DataContext* of the View. This allows you to start to bind the properties and commands of the ViewModel to the corresponding controls exposed in the View. To do that, you just add a reference to the *DataContext* using a procedural approach, as in the following code:

```
/// <summary>
/// Sets the data source.
/// </summary>
/// <param name="dataSource">The data source.</param>
public void SetViewModel(PersonModel dataSource)
{
    this.DataContext = dataSource;
}
```

Alternatively, you can add a reference to the *DataSource* by using an XAML declarative approach, as in the following XAML code:

```
<Window x:Class="MVVM.MainWindow"
        xmlns:vm="clr-namespace:MVVM"
        Title="MainWindow" Height="250" Width="250">
    <Window.DataContext>
        <vm:PersonViewModel />
    </Window.DataContext>
</Window.DataContext>
```

After accomplishing this step, you might safely leave the remaining work of creating the layout and assigning the binding of the ViewModel properties to the View Controls to a UI designer. Unfortunately, this example doesn't truly uncouple the View from the ViewModel, and it also introduces a constraint between the real ViewModel and the ViewModel the designer is using—because in this example, they are the same object. A better approach is to create a dummy ViewModel just for the designers so that they can continue to tweak the UI while you (or somebody else) can still work on the presentation logic for that view.

Of course, the properties, events, commands, and so on provided by the ViewModel represent a contract to the View. The View and ViewModel are not completely uncoupled; they are loosely coupled. If you define the contract up front, then you can mock out the ViewModel so that the UI designer can focus on the UI design while the developer focuses on implementing and unit testing the ViewModel.

Blendability: A Dummy ViewModel

Before you hand off the responsibility of creating the bindings to the designers, you can make their jobs easier while staying firmly on the MVVM track by introducing Microsoft Expression Blend and the Expression SDK into your process. By doing so, you can achieve *Blendability*. Of course, this is just a fancy term for enabling designers to see an accurate preview of their Views in Microsoft Visual Studio and/or Expression Blend.

Microsoft introduced a new namespace for WPF and Silverlight designers, which is available at *http://schemas.microsoft.com/expression/blend/2008*. Expression Blend is a UI design tool. It has an SDK that provides extensible *behaviors*. Behaviors are a way to package interactivity into re-usable components that can be dragged onto the UI. Expression Blend also provides a sample data feature that lets designers design the UI against dummy data. In terms of the MVVM pattern, the dummy data provides a mocked-up ViewModel.

The following code adds this namespace to the View using the *des* (for *design*) prefix:

```
xmlns:des="http://schemas.microsoft.com/expression/blend/2008"
des:DesignWidth="300" des:DesignHeight="300"
des:DataContext="{Binding SampleViewModel}"
```

The code *des:DataContext* simply allows you to specify a data context that will be used at design time; the real data context will be used at runtime. With this technique you can apply a dummy ViewModel at design time so that a designer can create the UI design based on dummy data, which of course will be replaced with real data at runtime. The previous code binds the design-time data context of the View to a class called *SampleViewModel*, Expression Blend creates a *SampleDataSource* object that's basically a collection of properties, which you can define, thus allowing the designer to create a dummy ViewModel with the same properties as the real ViewModel but using dummy data values.

To do that, you need to create an additional XAML file to act as the dummy ViewModel, and then populate it with dummy data (that closely reflects data from the real ViewModel). Designers use this dummy data file to proceed with the presentation logic development process. For example, the following is a sample XAML *Dummy ViewModel* for the Person view:

```
<vm:Customer
    xmlns:vm="clr-namespace:CRM.Domain.Domain;assembly=CRM.Domain"
    Title="Mr." FirstName="John" LastName="Smith"
    BirthDate="12/31/1970" IsActive="True">
    <vm:Customer.Contacts>
        <vm:Contact
            Name="Home Phone" ContactType="Phone"
            Number="111-11-11" IsDefault="True" />
        <vm:Contact
            Name="Office Phone" ContactType="Phone"
            Number="111-22-22" IsDefault="False" />
        <vm:Contact
            Name="Email" ContactType="Email"
            Number="john.smith@email.com" IsDefault="False" />
    </vm:Customer.Contacts>
    <vm:Customer.Addresses>
        <vm:Address
            AddressLine1="4 Main Street" City="New York"
            Country="USA" State="NY" ZipCode="11040" />
        <vm:Address
            AddressLine1="54 The Road" City="Seattle"
            Country="USA" State="WA" ZipCode="12000" />
    </vm:Customer.Addresses>
</vm:Customer>
```

The example creates a *Customer* model instance, because the ViewModel will expose one instance of this class with its related lists of contacts and addresses. The first line adds an instance of the *CRM.Domain.Customer* class using the *clr-namespace* declaration that is available in XAML; you use the same declaration to add a reference in the XAML-based View. Because the *Customer* model has some child collections required for the final View, those are also included and populated with some dummy data. This gives designers everything they need to create the View in Expression Blend.

Now that the designers have everything in place, they can bind the dummy ViewModel to the View and work on the binding process, the *DataTemplate*, and the styles without interrupting developer work on other parts of the application. The following code shows the binding syntax used in the XAML View to consume the previously created dummy data:

```xml
<UserControl x:Class="CRM.MVVM.WPF.DetailsView.CustomerDetails"
            <!--OMITTED -->
            xmlns:d="http://schemas.microsoft.com/expression/blend/2008"
            mc:Ignorable="d"
            d:DesignHeight="500" d:DesignWidth="500" DataContext="{Binding}"
            d:DataContext="{d:DesignData Source=/DesignData/CustomerSampleData.xaml}">
    <UserControl.Resources>

    <!--OMITTED -->

    <StackPanel>
      <TextBlock>First Name :</TextBlock>
      <TextBox Text="{Binding FirstName}"/>
      <TextBlock>Last Name :</TextBlock>
      <TextBox Text="{Binding LastName}"/>
      <TextBlock Text="Data of Birth :" />
      <DatePickerTextBox Text="{Binding Path=BirthDate.Date, StringFormat=\{0:d\}}" />
      <TextBlock>Is Active :</TextBlock>
      <CheckBox IsChecked="{Binding IsActive}" />
    </StackPanel>
```

Using this approach, the designer can work directly in either Expression Blend or Visual Studio to test the UI without actually running the application, because the UI render engine available in Expression Blend and Visual Studio can render the data at design time, as shown in Figure 6-3.

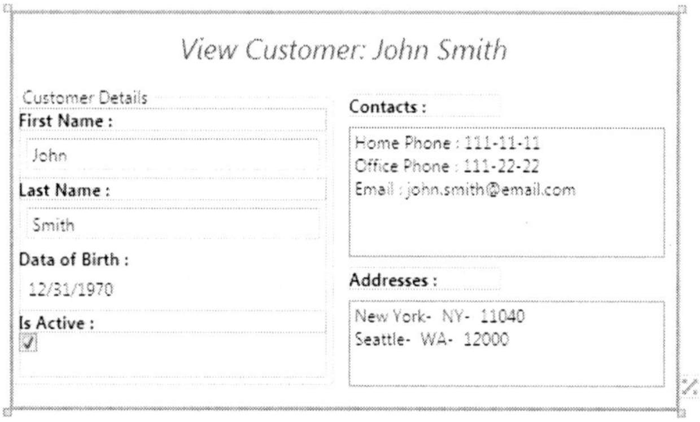

FIGURE 6-3 A design-time XAML View using the *DesignData* dummy ViewModel.

This approach looks pretty convenient at first glance, so it's worth noting a few possible disadvantages to using it.

First, if you intend to tweak the UI using the final ViewModel structure, you need to create a design-time ViewModel that represents all the properties, commands, and behaviors that you plan to expose in the final ViewModel. Second, you need to keep in mind that for huge ViewModels—for example a ViewModel that exposes 30 properties, plus commands and validation rules—creating a dummy ViewModel will take significant time. Finally, remember that it might not be possible to create a dummy value that matches each property, command, or behavior if your real ViewModel is complex, so you might need to think about other solutions. For example, you might create a complex dummy ViewModel composed of parent and child ViewModels. Such complexity might be difficult to represent using XAML markup.

The Model

As you might have noticed, this chapter has discussed the ViewModel—not the Model discussed in Chapter 3. In fact, the Model is a Domain Entity, declared and exposed in the Domain Model, and it should not be confused with the ViewModel, which is exposed in the View.

Expanding on that further, the Model is the entity in charge of moving data to and from the data store; that's the object known to the Data Layer and the Business Layer. By contrast, the ViewModel is the Model for a View—the part of Model exposed for that specific View, including the validation and behaviors needed in that specific UI circumstance, plus all the presentation logic. Figure 6-4 shows the flow of a Model and why it is often so different from a ViewModel.

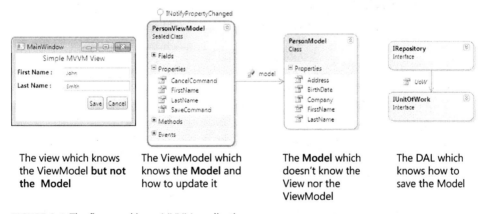

FIGURE 6-4 The flow used in an MVVM application.

Consider that you will *never* implement an *ICommand* in the Model, because the Model is not related to the UI, but you will probably expose the Model directly from the ViewModel to make it easier to create a custom DataTemplate for a specific Domain Entity from your Domain Model. This is a problem that we will analyze right now. A common mistake I've seen in MVVM implementations is that they pass the Model to the View from the ViewModel, so that (for example) the binding path of a *FirstName* property in the Person model would be exposed in the View in this way:

```
<TextBox Grid.Column="2" Grid.Row="1" Text="{Binding PersonModel.FirstName}" />
```

In my opinion, rather than letting the View bind to the property from the Model directly, the ViewModel should expose its own, separate property called *FirstName* that represents the *FirstName* of the Person Model:

```
<TextBox Grid.Column="2" Grid.Row="1" Text="{Binding FirstName}" />
```

Using this approach, the ViewModel becomes the Model for the View, masking the real Model. That improves the safety of the application because you're not exposing the whole Model directly to the View. In addition, it helps uncouple the View from the Model, because the View no longer needs to know anything about the Model directly.

Exposing the Model in the ViewModel

I have had this discussion in the past with many people. The solution of exposing the Model directly from the ViewModel, as a public property, and then binding it directly to the View is probably the easiest and fastest solution—but it doesn't represent the *purist* way of implementing a separated presentation pattern, in which the View should be only loosely coupled to the Model through a specific ViewModel.

Instead, the ViewModel should declare its own properties, hiding the specifics of the Model from the View. This provides the greatest flexibility, and it helps to prevent ViewModel-type issues from leaking into the Model classes.

You need to remember that if you plan to expose your Model properties directly into the View by exposing the Model as a property of the ViewModel, you should implement the *INotifyPropertyChanged* interface in the Domain Entity object, as well, and not only in the ViewModel; otherwise, when the View changes the Model, the ViewModel will not be able to see the change because the binding engine of WPF or Silverlight will raise a notification of the change.

On the other side, using the approach of rewriting each property of the Model (including child and parent relationships) inside the corresponding ViewModel is a daunting, time-consuming, and error-prone task, which also adds additional work in terms of testing and maintenance.

At this point, you're probably wondering which is the best approach. Quite honestly, there isn't a "best" approach; there are only different approaches to the same problem. If you want to expose the Model directly to the View so that you can easily write a *DataTemplate* that represents a Domain Entity, you will need to pollute your Domain Entities with the *INotifyPropertyChanged* interface. On the other hand, if you want to follow the purist way, you will wind up with a lot more code that must be written and tested. I would say that the "best" approach depends on the complexity and architecture of your application.

The Command in WPF and Silverlight

One of the most interesting features in WPF and Silverlight is the *ICommand* interface and how it works. The *ICommand* interface exposes *Execute* and *CanExecute* methods that let you control the command execution. By using the binding engine in WPF or Silverlight and the *ICommand* implementation, you are able to place a ViewModel that exposes *ICommand* commands in the View, and bind controls such as Button, Link, and so on to these commands. The *ICommand* lets you control command execution based on changes that might occur in the ViewModel. For example, you might enable the *Save* command on a View only after the ViewModel has fired the *OnPropertyChanged()* method at least once.

Usually, you will need to expose these commands in the ViewModel as public properties to properly create the binding between the View and the ViewModel. Exposing an *ICommand* property from the ViewModel allows the View to bind to the command proffered by the ViewModel. You can implement the *ICommand* interface in a number of ways. You also need to implement some presentation logic in your ViewModel to decide whether the command can or cannot be executed.

The common solution is to simply create a public property of type *ICommand* in the ViewModel with a private accessor that can evaluate some presentation logic inside the ViewModel itself. Another possible implementation is to create a custom class for each command that inherits from the *ICommand* interface and exposes it in the ViewModel—but of course, you would then need to create a custom command class for each command available in the application. You might think that this approach is time-consuming and counterproductive, but for shared commands, such as New, Save, Delete, Undo, or Redo, you will need to write the custom implementation of these commands only once. For other commands, you might wish to use the MVVM Command approach, which is explained in the next section.

A Workaround: An MVVM Command

Silverlight 3 had no support for the Commanding feature that is available in WPF. Unfortunately, Silverlight 4 doesn't support Commanding in the same way that WPF does, either. But thanks to the *ICommand* interface you saw earlier, you can easily bind a command to a Menu in Silverlight and recycle the same command to bind to a Button in WPF, without the need to rewrite any code.

Some third-party tools, such as Prism (Microsoft patterns & practices framework), MVVM Light Toolkit (Laurent Bugnion's framework), and Caliburn (CodePlex project) have their own implementations of *ICommand* that you can recycle in both Silverlight and WPF applications. The code you'll see in this section does the same thing by creating an *MVVMCommand* that you can expose in ViewModels rather than hard-coding an *ICommand* implementation.

First, create a new CRM.MVVM project, which will be the utility framework for the MVVM pattern. This is where the project stores some utility classes, which include MVVM command implementations for WPF and Silverlight.

The first class we will build is *MvvmCommand*, which must implement the *ICommand* interface. It defines a generic *Function<T>* for the *CanExecute* evaluation and a *Delegate<T>* for the *Execute* implementation. These methods are injected into the constructor of the command using the following code:

```
/// <summary>
///  Custom MVVM command
/// </summary>
public class MvvmCommand : ICommand
{
    private readonly Func<object, bool> canExecute;
    private readonly Action<object> executeAction;
    private bool canExecuteCache;

    /// <summary>
    /// Initializes a new instance of the <see cref="MvvmCommand"/> class.
    /// </summary>
    /// <param name="executeAction">The execute action.</param>
    /// <param name="canExecute">The can execute.</param>
    public MvvmCommand(Action<object> executeAction, Func<object, bool> canExecute)
    {
        this.executeAction = executeAction;
        this.canExecute = canExecute;
    }
}
```

Of course, this type of implementation forces you to implement the execution logic of the *Execute* and the *CanExecute* method outside of the command itself—probably directly into the ViewModel that exposes them.

First, you implement the *CanExecute* method, which evaluates whether a command can or cannot be executed. This action is supported by both the WPF and Silverlight engines but in different ways. For example, WPF has a Command Manager class that re-evaluates the UI (and of course, the bound ViewModel) every time the UI changes. The UI change fires the re-evaluation of the *CanExecute* action automatically. In contrast, the Silverlight engine doesn't have a command manager, so you need to implement the re-evaluation yourself.

The following code represents a simple *CanExecute* implementation that raises an event every time the command is re-evaluated:

```
/// Defines the method that determines whether the command
/// can execute in its current state.
/// </summary>
/// <param name="parameter">Data used by the command.  If the command
/// does not require data to be passed, this object can be set to null.</param>
/// <returns>
/// true if this command can be executed; otherwise, false.
/// </returns>
public bool CanExecute(object parameter)
{
    if (CanExecuteChanged != null)
    {
        CanExecuteChanged(this, new EventArgs());
    }
    return canExecute(parameter);
}

public event EventHandler CanExecuteChanged;
```

Now that you can evaluate command execution, you can simply associate the execution delegate provided in the constructor to the one required by the *ICommand* interface, as follows:

```
/// <summary>
/// Defines the method to be called when the command is invoked.
/// </summary>
/// <param name="parameter">Data used by the command.  If the command
/// does not require data to be passed, this object can be set to null.</param>
public void Execute(object parameter)
{
    executeAction(parameter);
}
```

As it is set up here, you can declare a command on the ViewModel with a private accessor and assign two lambda expressions to get a concrete implementation of the MVVM command in this way:

```
public sealed class PersonViewModel : BaseViewModel<Person>
{
    public ICommand SavePerson { get; private set; }

    /// <summary>
    /// Initializes a new instance of the <see cref="PersonViewModel"/> class.
```

```
/// </summary>
/// <param name="model">The model.</param>
public PersonViewModel(Person model)
    : base(model){}

/// <summary>
/// Inits the commands.
/// </summary>
private void InitCommands()
{
    SavePerson = new MvvmCommand(
        (parm) =>
            {
                // execute
                PersonService.Save(model);
            },
        (parm) =>
            {
                // canExecute, can save if
                // the model is valid ...
                return model.IsValid;
            });
}
}
```

Now, every time you change the *Person* (in this specific case), the UI will re-evaluate the *Save* command, and if the *Person* model is not valid, it will disable the Save button. You need only a final tweak to fix the problem of Silverlight not having a Command Manager.

Re-evaluate *ICommand* Execution

What we've done up until now is pretty cool, flexible, and testable; we can create a generic *MvvmCommand*, expose it as an *ICommand* interface object and declare the code to execute and to evaluate the execution using the anonymous delegate, which is also fancy and pretty readable.

At this point, you'll probably try to create a basic ViewModel object that exposes a couple of properties and an *ICommand* property, like the one in the following listing, and you'll bind these properties to a View. What you want is to enable the *FormatCommand* property only if the text in the *TextBox* is not null.

The *CanExecute* method of an *ICommand* object is executed only when the DataBinding engine creates the binding between the UI element and the command, and then the command execution is re-evaluated only if something changes and the *CommandManager* is listening for that change. For example, when you change the text in the *TextBox*, the *CommandManager* is unaware of the change, and it doesn't update the command, so the Button remains disabled.

If the code were not in a ViewModel but in the code-behind for a specific Window or UserControl, you could call the static method *CommandManager.InvalidateRequerySuggested* method that raises the *RequerySuggested* event, which then re-evaluates all the commands inside the *CommandManager*. Unfortunately, if you call this method inside the ViewModel object, it simply doesn't work because you don't have access directly to the View *CommandManager* object.

Another big disadvantage of using the *CommandManager* is that it doesn't re-evaluate just the execution of one command; instead it re-evaluates all the commands attached to the *CommandBinding* collection.

A possible alternative is to manually re-evaluate the command each time the *OriginalText* property changes, such as in the following code:

```
public string OriginalText
{
    get { return originalText; }
    set
    {
        originalText = value;
        OnPropertyChanged(vm => vm.OriginalText);
        (FormatCommand as MvvmCommand).OnCanExecuteChanged();
    }
}
```

Another interesting alternative would be to make the command aware of changes that might happen in the ViewModel and re-execute the *OnCanExecuteChanged()* method if this "change" happens in the ViewModel. In other words, that means making the *ICommand* listen for the *PropertyChanged* event raised by the ViewModel.

The ViewModel

Recall that the classic definition of a ViewModel in the MVVM pattern is that the *"ViewModel is the Model provided for the View,"* which is not necessarily sufficient to describe the power this object might acquire during an application's development process.

The ViewModel should satisfy four principal requirements:

- Provide the data that must be exposed in the View
- Provide a set of commands available in the View
- Implement the *INotifyPropertyChanged* interface
- Implement the *IDataErrorInfo* interface

Of course, not all ViewModel implementations must satisfy all four requirements. Depending on the situation, it might not be necessary for a ViewModel to expose a set of *ICommand* commands, or implement the *IDataErrorInfo* interface (used for UI validation), or the *INotifyPropertyChanged* interface (which raises notifications about UI changes). The implementation of any given ViewModel depends upon specific use cases. But all ViewModels will expose at least some values.

The previous section discussed the pros and cons of exposing the Model from the ViewModel. For explanatory purposes, I will expose the sample application Domain Entities directly from the ViewModel in the View—but that doesn't mean that you *must* expose data in your ViewModel using this approach.

The next sections explain how you should implement the four ViewModel requirements and how to create some custom base ViewModels that you can then recycle in your future MVVM applications.

The *INotifyPropertyChanged* Interface

The *INotifyPropertyChanged* interface has been available since the .NET Framework version 2.0. It resides in the System.dll and is exposed through the namespace *System. ComponentModel*. *INotifyPropertyChanged* provides a mechanism for notifying a client or any other listener that the value of a property (or of an entire object) has changed. It exposes a *PropertyChanged* event that requires a custom implementation in inheriting classes. If you bind an object that implements this interface to an XAML datasource, for example, the View will receive a notification each time the object changes. In the same way, if you bind such an object to a Windows Form data source, the same behavior will occur without the need to modify any code because of the changed data source.

At this point, you can think of any object that implements the interface *INotifyPropertyChanged* as an *Observable object,* which is an abstract object type that you'll create here for your MVVM toolkit. The only requirement is that the observable object must implement the *INotifyPropertyChanged* interface, which is abstract because it's a base class; you don't want it to be used directly. Finally, you want to define the property that has changed using lambda expressions.

To start, create a new class in the CRM.MVVM project and call it **ObservableObject**, as shown here:

```
public abstract class ObservableObject<T> : INotifyPropertyChanged
```

Every object that implements this interface will use itself as *<T>*. In this way, you can now use a lambda expression trick to auto-resolve the property name. The next step is the interface implementation:

```
#region Implementation of INotifyPropertyChanged

/// <summary>
/// Occurs when a property value changes.
/// </summary>
public event PropertyChangedEventHandler PropertyChanged;

/// <summary>
/// Called when [property changed].
/// </summary>
/// <param name="property">The property.</param>
protected virtual void OnPropertyChanged(Expression<Func<T, object>> property)
{
    if (property == null || property.Body == null)
    {
        return;
    }

    var memberExp = property.Body as MemberExpression;
    if (memberExp == null)
    {
        return;
    }

    PropertyChangedEventHandler handler = PropertyChanged;
    if (handler != null)
    {
        handler(this, new PropertyChangedEventArgs(memberExp.Member.Name));
    }
}
}

#endregion
```

The preceding code declares a *PropertyChanged* event, which requires a
PropertyChangedEventArgs argument that holds the name of the property that has
changed. Then we have the signature of the *OnPropertyChanged* delegate, which is the
method that will be called each time a property changes. Note that this code doesn't use a
compiled lambda expression result (which is slower), because we want to read only the value
of the body of the lambda expression; this technique will not affect the runtime performance.
If there are any subscribers to the event, you raise the event, including the property name.

Now we can implement this class in our base ViewModel in the following way:

```
public class BaseViewModel<T> : ObservableObject<BaseViewModel<T>> where T : class
{
    public T model;

    /// <summary>
    /// Gets or sets the model.
    /// </summary>
    /// <value>The model.</value>
    public T Model
```

```
            {
                get { return model; }
                set
                {
                    if (model == value)
                    {
                        return;
                    }
                    model = value;
                    OnPropertyChanged(vm => vm.Model);
                }
            }
        }
    }
```

This example shows a base ViewModel class that requires a generic *<T>* model. This is the model that you will expose in the View using the XAML *DataBind* engine. If the model changes, it will notify the UI by firing the *OnPropertyChanged* event.

You can do the same thing with simple properties such as a string or integer property exposed through the ViewModel.

The *IDataErrorInfo* Interface

The *IDataErrorInfo* interface also resides in the *System.ComponentModel* namespace. It's intended to provide specific error information for an object bound to a client interface (a View). This interface has been exposed by the .NET Framework since version 1.0 (although with a different structure), but it became famous only when WPF and Silverlight appeared. However, you can easily use it in a Windows client or ASP.NET application to implement data validation in a View.

The interface exposes two properties: *Error* and *Item*. The *Error* property represents the current validation error. This is most commonly implemented in the client, so you won't implement this property in the sample toolkit, because you'll display validation errors using the XAML data template, instead.

The *Item* property is invoked each time an item in the View (which has validation enabled, so a change triggers the validation engine) changes its value and/or requires validation.

A simple implementation of this interface in the base ViewModel should look something like this:

```
/// <summary>
/// Gets the <see cref="System.String"/> with the specified column name.
/// </summary>
/// <value></value>
public virtual string this[string columnName]
{
    get
    {
        var errorMessage = string.Empty;
```

```
            switch (columnName)
            {
                case "Model":
                    if (this.Model == null)
                    {
                        errorMessage = "The View can't be bound to an empty model.";
                    }
                    break;
            }
            return errorMessage;
        }
    }
```

It should be *virtual* so that you can override the implementation in each concrete ViewModel. For example a *PersonViewModel* might have different validation rules. This process is not terribly productive, it's time-consuming, and it's probably redundant, because you might already have some validation rules applied to the underlying model.

A smarter way to accomplish this task is to use the Microsoft Enterprise Library that you saw in Chapter 5, "The Business Layer," to self-validate both the ViewModel and the underlying model, which already has validation rules.

To do that, you first need a *ViewModelValidator* class that you can call whenever you need to validate a ViewModel property or validate an entire object. The Validation Application Block (VAB) provided with the Enterprise Library offers a neat and easy way to validate an object, so I suggest that you use it, and verify that any validation errors that occur are related to the property we are trying to validate. Here's the code for validating a field:

```
    public sealed class ViewModelValidator
    {
        /// <summary>
        /// Validates the field.
        /// </summary>
        /// <param name="entity">The entity.</param>
        /// <param name="field">The field.</param>
        /// <returns></returns>
        public static string ValidateField<T>(T entity, string field)
        {
            var validationResults =
                ValidationFactory.CreateValidator<T>().Validate(entity);
            var errorMessage = new StringBuilder();
            // if the entity is valid we don't go ahead
            if (validationResults.IsValid)
            {
                return errorMessage.ToString();
            }
            // verify that the errors are for this field
            var errors = validationResults.Where(x => x.Key == field);
            if (errors.Count() > 0)
            {
```

```
            foreach (var validationResult in errors)
            {
                errorMessage.AppendLine(validationResult.Message);
            }
        }
        // return the error message as a string with \r\n
        return errorMessage.ToString();
    }
}
```

And this is the change in the base ViewModel:

```
/// <summary>
/// Gets the <see cref="System.String"/> with the specified column name.
/// </summary>
/// <value></value>
public virtual string this[string columnName]
{
    get
    {
        return ViewModelValidator.ValidateField(this, columnName);
    }
}
```

Now the trick is to bind the ViewModel to a View and create a specific visual method—for example a *TextBox*—to display any errors generated during the validation process. Figure 6-5 presents a functional validation style that uses a WPF *TextBox*.

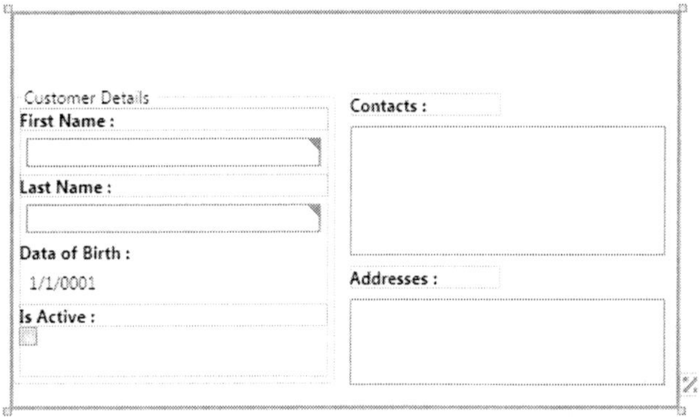

FIGURE 6-5 Validation template applied on a WPF *TextBox*.

To see more information about the validation template, examine the *Validation.ErrorTemplate* attached property. This property lets you define a specific template for a control to display a validation error.

Of course, to raise the validation in the first place, you need to define the binding as shown in the following code example, specifying the *ValidatesOnDataErrors* and *ValidateOnExceptions* attributes to make the binding engine aware of the validation availability in the *DataContext*:

```
<TextBox Text="{
  Binding ValidatesOnDataErrors=True,
  Path=FirstName,
  ValidatesOnExceptions=True
}">
</TextBox>
```

DataTemplate in WPF and Silverlight

Another important aspect of the WPF/Silverlight UI engine is the *DataTemplate*, which describes how to render data that is bound to a control by specifying how the data will be rendered. Windows Forms doesn't have an easy way to customize the items exposed by a list control, such as a *Listbox*, so you had to create a custom property in the Model exposed in the *DataSource* of the control in order to use it as a *Display* property of that control.

With WPF or Silverlight, however, you can easily bind a *Person* class to a *UserControl*, and bind a collection property from that class, such as a list of addresses, to a *Listbox*. By customizing the data template, you can cause the *ListBox* UI to look like a simple *Grid* and avoid using a more complex *Grid* control. The following code uses a *DataTemplate* to display three properties of an *Address* entity in a *ListBox*:

```
<ListBox ItemsSource="{Binding Contacts}"
    Grid.Column="5" Grid.ColumnSpan="3"
    Grid.Row="2" Grid.RowSpan="3">
    <ListBox.ItemTemplate>
        <DataTemplate>
            <StackPanel Orientation="Horizontal">
                <TextBlock Text="{Binding Name}" />
                <TextBlock Text=" : " />
                <TextBlock Text="{Binding Number}" />
            </StackPanel>
        </DataTemplate>
    </ListBox.ItemTemplate>
</ListBox>
```

Another interesting approach would be to have an *IList<ICommand>* exposed in the ViewModel. Then, using the *DataTemplate*, you could create a dynamic list of buttons or a list of commands in a Command Bar, resulting in an extremely dynamic View.

DataTemplate and MVVM

Why is the *DataTemplate* so important for the MVVM Pattern? The principal purpose of the MVVM pattern—or more accurately, one of the primary reasons for using the MVVM pattern—is to separate presentation logic from UI logic so that your ViewModels can be loosely coupled and reusable. If you use a *DataTemplate* to display the data exposed by the ViewModel in the View, you'll wind up with more flexibility in the future for changing and adapting that View to a new design requirement or to a new client technology, such as from WPF to Silverlight.

Also, because a *DataTemplate* is essentially a View without code-behind, you can bind the UI directly against a ViewModel and apply a *DataTemplate*, which then becomes the View to the ViewModel.

Refer back to Figure 6-3, which represents a Customer Details View bound to a *CustomerViewModel*. How many times are you likely to use this View? In a real-world CRM application, you would probably use this View several times; for example, to represent a selected customer, to create a new customer, to display the customer details in an order view, and so on.

You can see that this approach could be very time-consuming; you would need to apply the same validation rules and write the same XAML view repeatedly. Using a *DataTemplate*, you can create a simple *UserControl* in both Silverlight and WPF, bind it to a *CustomerViewModel*, and then add a reference to that *DataTemplate* to any View that requires it, thus saving time and making the code more reusable.

WeakEvents and Messages

If you are familiar with event programming with .NET, you might already know what an event is and how painful it can be to create and destroy events attached to a specific form.

With WPF and .NET Framework 4, Microsoft has introduced a new type of event called *WeakEvent*, which implements the Weak Event design pattern—a mechanism that is able to self-manage the event subscription and cancellation process. You can accomplish the same result in Silverlight, as you'll see later in this section.

The *WeakEvent* Pattern

In the old-fashioned style of managing events, the lifecycle of an object that listens for an event (the *listener*) might be different than expected because it's driven by the lifecycle of the object raising the event (the *source*). In this case, the only possible solution is to remove the listener from the source *declaratively*, by detaching the event handler from the source.

With .NET 4 you can now use two different objects to implement the *WeakEvent* pattern: *WeakEventManager*, a class that you should inherit to create a custom event manager, and *IWeakEventListener*, an interface that any listener for a weak event should implement.

Figure 6-6 displays the basic implementation of the *WeakEvent* pattern in .NET.

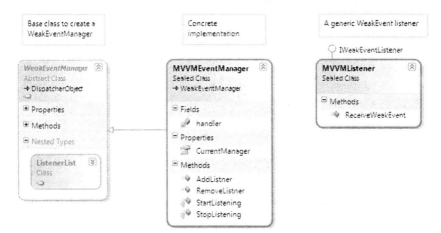

FIGURE 6-6 *WeakEvent* pattern implementation.

As illustrated in Figure 6-6, this implementation is both time-consuming and verbose, especially when you realize that this implementation should be applied to every event that you want to listen for from the UI.

At this point, you will probably want to move to a more generic solution (available in the downloadable companion source code for this book) and create a factory that is able to subscribe and remove listeners to an event using lambda expressions and delegates. The final result looks like this:

```
MyEventFactory.Listen<MyEventHandler>(
    () =>
    {
        // implement event here …
    });
```

Unfortunately, that solution runs into another .NET problem, because it's difficult (if not impossible) to subscribe and unsubscribe to an event—even a weak event—using lambda expression syntax. So you might want to skip this altogether and consider adopting a more reliable solution: the Messaging pattern.

The *EventAggregator* Pattern

I always followed with pleasure any guidance provided by Microsoft's patterns & practices team, especially the Smart Client Software Factory (SCSF). I know it was designed for Windows Forms, but it was very cool at that time (circa 2004/2005), and in fact, the Publisher/Subscriber pattern is still available and implemented in Prism, the composite UI application framework for WPF and Silverlight.

The best part of that application block was the way it managed events in a thread-safe manner, without affecting either performance or the UI. (Remember that in Windows Forms and also in WPF or Silverlight, you are not allowed to listen in the UI for events raised by another thread.)

The Message pattern follows this simple logic. You have a *sender* and a *subscriber*, both of which can send and receive messages. These messages contain some data, of course, and might be sent at any time in the lifecycle of the application. If you think about it, this is nothing more than an alternative solution for the Event pattern.

In Prism and SCSF, Microsoft introduced the *EventAggregator*, which is a powerful event manager that can subscribe to any type of event and call an action every time that event is raised. This object follows the Message pattern. Its only requirement is that you must implement your events using a specific base class. Figure 6-7 shows how the *EventAggregator* works.

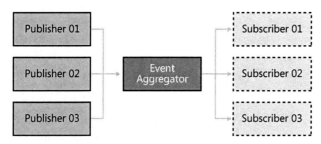

FIGURE 6-7 The *EventAggregator* pattern.

The *EventAggregator* will contain code that subscribes to an event and code that forwards an event to subscribers. The implementation should look something like this:

```
// send a "Message"
var event = EventAggregator.Get<MyEvent>();
event.Send("parameters");

// subscribe to the "Message"
var event = EventAggregator.Get<MyEvent>();
event.Subscribe(
    () =>
    {
        // do something here
    });
```

This solves a couple of problems: you no longer need to worry about resources being kept alive by the listeners, and it also introduces a standardized communication pattern. Like any other pattern, the Message pattern has some requirements that you must satisfy in your design, such as:

- You need to register the message somewhere. Usually this step is accomplished by a *bootstrapper* or an *initializer* method in your UI.

- After registering the message, you must keep the aggregator alive that will notify listeners for that message. This is a perfect requirement for an Inversion of Control container. In this case, I usually use the Service Locator pattern.

- Just as Prism and other composite UI application frameworks do, you should add constraints to your messages to make them discoverable and unique. It might be difficult to distinguish a message that carries a general string value.

Dialogs and Modal Pop-Ups

One of the more complex tasks that you need to accomplish when using the MVVM pattern is to keep a *dialog* open between the user and a View, by means of a dialog window or a modal pop-up. This task is difficult not because of any difficulties in creating a dialog view in WPF or Silverlight, but because the loosely-coupled design that distinguishes the MVVM pattern makes the task hard to accomplish while keeping the View separate from the presentation logic.

Before exploring how you go about doing this, I want to show you the difference between a *MessageBox* displayed in WPF or Silverlight and a modal pop-up. Usually, a dialog window is a particular view that pops up in front of any other view, and prevents users from continuing program execution until the modal view receives a specific input or confirmation. This type of window, which includes both the *MessageBox* and the *FolderDialogBox* is called a *modal dialog*. Other windows, such as the *FindAndReplace* dialog that is available in most editors also appears in front of any other view, but it's not modal, because it allows you to edit the content of the view below. This type of window is called a *modeless dialog*.

WPF offers a set of default dialogs that are commonly used in applications. Some display a message to users and require a response, which is usually some combination of "Yes," "No," and "Cancel." This type of dialog is known as a *MessageBox*; it is a classic modal dialog box. Other types are the *OpenFileDialog*, *SaveFileDialog*, and so on. These types of dialogs prevent users from proceeding with the main application until they complete some action inside the modal view. After that action has been completed, execution returns to the original application, which reads the result from the dialog view.

You can also create a custom View that might act as a dialog just by launching the View with the *ShowDialog* command in C# or Visual Basic .NET.

Modal View in MVVM

Using the MVVM pattern, the common approach for showing a dialog view won't work because the dialog code runs inside the View, and thus resides in the UI logic. But in MVVM, such code should execute in the presentation logic, in the ViewModel code.

There are various approaches to accomplish dialog display. By examining the code in the available open source MVVM toolkits, such as MVVM Light, Prism, and Caliburn, you will discover that each one uses a different approach, but they are all efficient. It's up to you to understand and decide which one is the best for you and your needs.

Modal Service

The first example you'll see here is called the "service approach." Using this method, you create a service in charge of managing the dialog views. The general idea is to create some code, (a service in this case), that acts as a *ModalService*, which is able to create and destroy any type of dialog and return the dialog result. Here's some simplified pseudocode for the service contract:

```
public interface IDialogService
{
    bool? ShowDialogMessage(string title, string message);
    bool? ShowDialogView(object view, object viewModel);
    void ShowMessage(string title, string message);
    void ShowView(object view, object viewModel);
}
```

One possible way to implement this service is with an Inversion of Control framework that renders the service directly in your ViewModels. At this point, you can create a command that can show a *MessageBox* and wait until it returns a *Boolean* value (*true* if the user confirmed some action, *false* for cancellation, and *null* if the user closed the *MessageBox* without answering).

```
private IDialogService dialogService;

public ICommand SavePerson { get; private set; }

/// <summary>
/// Inits the commands.
/// </summary>
private void InitCommands()
{
    ShowMessage = new MVVM.Commanding.MvvmCommand(
```

```
(sender) =>
    {
        var result =
        dialogService.ShowDialogMessage("Confirm?", "This is a confirm message.");
        if (result.HasValue && result.Value)
        {
            // do something
        }
    },
(sender) =>
{
    return true;
});
}
```

I like this approach because it doesn't require a lot of effort and doesn't pollute the View or the UI logic with the code required to implement the dialog. Of course, this is just a starting point—if you plan to use this approach, you should keep in mind that:

- You might need a return value of a different type, such as a selected value.

- The dialog result might raise a message or fire an event that updates the parent ViewModel/View.

- The dialog might need to listen for additional messages and update its status (for example, a progress bar dialog that responds to a long-running task update).

A Mediator Approach

The WPF Disciples, a group composed of developers passionately interested in WPF technology and the MVVM pattern, propose another interesting approach.

The mediator approach emulates the Mediator pattern, which tries to encapsulate the communication logic between two or more objects into an external class, called *Mediator*. The Mediator pattern involves two major steps: subscription and notification. For subscription, any object can subscribe to the mediator, making the mediator aware of the subscriber. The mediator then listens to notifications raised by the subscribed objects and reacts based on some specific business logic.

In MVVM, you can use the *Mediator* to accomplish the messaging task; Views subscribe to a mediator, and the mediator then listens and redirects messages raised by the subscribed Views. This approach is similar to the common event approach, wherein a listener registers a delegate to an event and waits to be notified when the event is raised by a caller. In Prism, the composite application framework released by the patterns & practices team, the

EventAggregator, uses the Mediator pattern in conjunction with *Action<T>* and *WeakEvents* to accomplish this task, as shown in the following:

```
// Event aggregator in PRISM
// subscription
eventAggregator.Get<MyEvent>().Subscribe(
    (message) =>
        {
            // some code
        });
// sending a notification
eventAggregator.Get<MyEvent>().SendMessage(MyMessage);
```

You can use the Mediator pattern in conjunction with a dialog service, because together they accomplish two different tasks. By using the Mediator pattern, you don't need to wait for the dialog result, because the subscriber will be notified when the dialog is complete; conversely, a plain dialog service simply locks the application while waiting for an answer or a user input.

Inversion of Control with MVVM

If you are planning to build your own MVVM facilities you should also consider how you plan to bootstrap the application; how you want to load common services and containers; and how to keep the MVVM triad and other objects involved in your application alive. You should also contemplate how to manage the loose coupling between objects and managing their dependencies during creation.

Toward the beginning of this chapter, in the section, "The View," you learned how to bind a data context for a View to a design-time ViewModel, just to provide enough flexibility so designers can continue the process of developing the UI part of our MVVM application without requiring a finalized ViewModel. But this approach fixes only part of the problem, because you haven't yet seen how to *inject* a ViewModel at runtime for the View. You also haven't seen how to initialize the ViewModel chain dependencies properly. Using Inversion of Control (IoC), you will avoid having a dependency between the View and the ViewModel, because that will be injected at runtime by the IoC framework itself.

If you use an IoC container, such as Microsoft Unity, you can sort out the bootstrap problem by using it as an application bootstrapper. The section "Inversion of Control" on page 44, covered what an IoC container is and how it should be used. Figure 6-7 shows the normal flow used by an MVVM application bootstrapped by an IoC container.

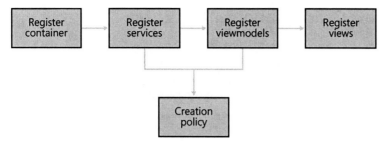

FIGURE 6-8 An MVVM application bootstrapping sequence.

The normal flow would follow a sequence like this:

- Activate the IoC container
- Register common Services and Utilities using policies to define lifecycles
- Register ViewModels and relative dependencies to navigation services and utilities
- Register Views and final injection of the corresponding ViewModel

Using that sequence, in pseudocode, you can now orchestrate an MVVM triad as follows:

```
// retrieve a ViewModel
var vm = iocContainer.Resolve<IPersonsViewModel>();
vm.InitializeData();

// resolve the View
var view = iocContainer.Resolve<IPersonsView>();
// data bind
view.Datacontext = vm;

// open the view using an INavigator service
var service = iocContainer.Resolve<INavigator>();
service.ShowView(view);
```

Some of the MVVM frameworks already available in the .NET community use this type of approach to resolve a chain of dependencies between the Services, the ViewModels, and the Views, just by resolving a specific View that fires the resolving process in the IoC container.

Sample Code

In this chapter's sample code section, you'll see how to solve some common problems that you might encounter while working on a WPF or Silverlight LOB application, which would typically be composed of a specific set of controls and UI components. For example, you might need to know how to build a Ribbon control within MVVM, or how to create some basic ViewModels that you can use throughout the application, and so on.

The first issue you'll tackle here is plugging a Microsoft Office Ribbon control into WPF.

The Microsoft Office Ribbon and MVVM

If you plan to work with the Microsoft Office Ribbon on a WPF application, the first step is to go to the CodePlex project for WPF (*http://wpf.codeplex.com*) and find the Office Ribbon section. You will need to go to the Office UI License site at the provided URL and accept the license agreement with regard to using the WPF Ribbon on your application; then you need to download the latest version of the Ribbon and reference the Ribbon DLL in your MVVM application.

More Information If you're not familiar with the Ribbon control, you will find the section of MSDN dedicated to guidance and tutorials on how to use the WPF Ribbon control extremely useful. You can find it at *http://msdn.microsoft.com/en-us/library/cc872782.aspx*.

This section focuses on how you can plug an Office Ribbon into an MVVM application, not on how to build a Ribbon control, as that is beyond the scope of this book.

Note From the Ribbon project website, you can also download some beta Visual Studio templates that help you build a specific View or WPF application that integrates the Ribbon control.

The following code shows how you can create a simple Ribbon tab that contains a Ribbon group pane containing a Ribbon button control.

```
<ribbon:RibbonGroup x:Name="Group1"
   Header="Group1">
   <ribbon:RibbonButton x:Name="Button1"
      LargeImageSource="Images\LargeIcon.png"
      Label="Button1" />
</ribbon:RibbonGroup>
```

Because the Ribbon control fully implements the *Commanding* binding, you can control the status and the execution of a Ribbon control by accessing its *Command* property, as you would with a normal Button control.

```
<ribbon:RibbonButton x:Name="Button1" Command="MyMVVMCommand"
```

At this point, the Ribbon control will behave just like any other UI control bound to an MVVM *Command* that implements the *ICommand* interface.

Another suggested approach is to bind each Ribbon item to a specific *DataContext* item, and bind each property of the *DataContext* item to the corresponding properties of the Ribbon controls, using, for example, WPF styles. This will give you more control over the Ribbon behaviors.

```
<ribbon:RibbonButton DataContext="{x:Static data:WordModel.Cut}" />

<!-RibbonControl style -->
<Style x:Key="RibbonControlStyle">
   <Setter Property="ribbon:RibbonControlService.Label"
      Value="{Binding Label}" />
   <Setter Property="ribbon:RibbonControlService.LargeImageSource"
      Value="{Binding LargeImage}" />
```

Here's the suggested way to define a style for a Ribbon button and bind the corresponding *Command*.

```
<!-- RibbonButton -->
<Style TargetType="{x:Type ribbon:RibbonButton}"
   BasedOn="{StaticResource RibbonControlStyle}">
   <Setter Property="Command" Value="{Binding Command}" />
</Style>
```

Using code like this, you can keep the *ICommand* interface as the Ribbon implementation pattern and bind the *Command* to the Ribbon control using *TwoWay* binding, so that the Ribbon state will always be re-evaluated based on what the UI state.

> **Note** The WPF Ribbon SDK includes an interesting example that illustrates how to populate the Ribbon control within the constraints of MVVM, by using a collection of commands bound to the entire Ribbon control.

Summary

The Model View ViewModel pattern is based on the Presentation Model pattern introduced by Martin Fowler, but it has a specific implementation related to WPF and Silverlight. The pattern involves three components that can be summarized as the View, the Model, and the ViewModel.

The core engine of an MVVM application is the ViewModel object, which contains the presentation logic of the application and acts as an intermediary to bind the Model to the View. A standard ViewModel should implement the *INotifyPropertyChanged* interface to be compatible with the WPF and Silverlight binding engine and should implement the *IDataErrorInfo* interface so it can notify the UI about validation errors. Usually, the ViewModel is in charge of exposing and managing its *Commands* bound to the View.

Using the WPF engine, you can build a very flexible MVVM application—especially if you include the *DataTemplate* and the styles provided with the UI engine. To notify and interact with users, you can use Dialogs, Modal Views, and Pop-ups; each should be used appropriately for specific UI design requirements.

Because of its *dependency* design, the MVVM pattern works extremely well when orchestrated with an IoC container such as Unity, which lets you create a simple workflow to manage the application.

Chapter 7
MVVM Frameworks and Toolkits

Although the Model View ViewModel (MVVM) pattern is not yet a famous presentation pattern along the lines of Model View Presenter (MVP) and Model View Controller (MVC), it is an evolution of these patterns and rapidly gaining fame in the .NET community. Despite not having been around very long, there are already a number of frameworks and toolkits that you can use to implement MVVM with Window Presentation Foundation (WPF), Silverlight, or Windows Phone 7.

This chapter discusses some of the more common MVVM frameworks available in the .NET environment. You'll see how they can solve many of the problems discussed in the previous chapters related to presentation logic in an MVVM application—most of which occur because WPF and Silverlight are two different technologies. The chapter also briefly explores a technology called "Prism," that the Microsoft patterns & practices team has spent a lot of time and effort developing.

These frameworks not only explain how to implement the MVVM pattern in WPF and Silverlight; they also provide a set of tools and facilities with which you can build a modular and very functional application.

MVVM Toolkits

When I look for an MVVM toolkit, I usually prepare a list of requirements that I want the framework to handle easily, and then I try to determine whether the framework I'm evaluating satisfies my requirements. The MVVM pattern has a strict set of core requirements for basic implementation, such as the *INotifyPropertyChanged* interface implementation, UI validation, and commanding support. In addition, there is a set of advanced functionalities more generally related to a UI application, including Views testability, messaging between views, event handling, and so on.

The previous chapter showed that it is not easy to implement an MVVM command that you can use easily in both WPF and Silverlight, in the same way. Usually, this will require having to rewrite the code, because the two technologies handle the *ICommand* interface in different ways. It is not also easy to expose the Model in the ViewModel without having to write redundant code, because of the lack of automation in the base classes.

This chapter examines all of these requirements by discussing a set of MVVM Toolkits and facilities that you can use to quickly resolve these problems.

> **Note** The three major MVVM Toolkits that are introduced in the following section are available from the .NET community. You can download and use them more or less immediately in your projects. But the availability of such prebuilt toolkits should not prevent you from implementing your own toolkit. It's also worth noting that these three are not the only available toolkits. There are other, less mature toolkits on CodePlex and other .NET community sites that you can try out and use. The three presented here have rich documentation and active communities, which makes them good starting points for practice and mastery of the MVVM pattern.

MVVM Light Toolkit, by Laurent Bugnion

Laurent Bugnion is a great developer the recipient of a Most Valuable Person (MVP) award from Microsoft for his work related to Silverlight technology. Three or four years ago, Laurent wrote an MVVM toolkit for WPF that has evolved to support Silverlight and Windows Phone 7, as well. That toolkit is now called the MVVM Light Toolkit.

As of the beginning of 2011, the toolkit is now at version 3. It has full support for WPF, Silverlight, and Windows Phone 7. You can download it from *http://www.galasoft.ch/mvvm/getstarted/*. MVVM Light Toolkit integrates nicely with both Visual Studio 2010 and Microsoft Expression Blend.

After installing the toolkit on your development machine, you'll see that the installation added some extensions to Microsoft Visual Studio 2010 and Expression Blend, which gain new WPF, Silverlight, and Windows Phone 7 project templates and code-snippets.

> **Note** In Visual Studio 2010, a code-snippet is a special file with a .snippet extension that works with IntelliSense, giving you a quick and easy way to insert ready-made snippets of code into your projects.

Figure 7-1 shows this integration in Visual Studio 2010 and Expression Blend.

Integration with Expression Blend 3 and 4   Integration with Visual Studio 2008 and 2010

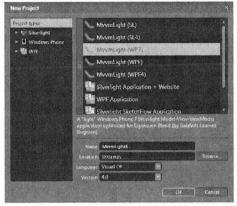 

FIGURE 7-1 MVVM Toolkit integration with Visual Studio 2010 and Expression Blend.

The toolkit provides the following features for writing an MVVM application

- A *ViewModelBase* class that you can use for any ViewModel object

- A *Messenger* class that implements the Publisher/Subscriber pattern as well as a full set of messaging components, such as *NotificationMessages*, *DialogMessages*, *PropertyChangedMessages*, and more

- A flexible *RelayCommand* (MVVM Command) that works for both WPF and Silverlight

- Helpers and facilities to work with the Dispatcher of WPF and Silverlight for multi-threading UI integration, Expression Blend integration, Item templates, project templates in Visual Studio, and more

MEFedMVVM

MEFedMVVM is a library for building Managed Extensibility Framework (MEF) applications using Silverlight or WPF; it provides a set of base classes and components through which you can implement the MVVM pattern with the help of MEF.

> **Note** MEF is a library that is exposed in the System.ComponentModel.Composition assembly that addresses the problem of designing extensible and composable applications. You already saw how MEF works in the previous chapters, especially during the discussion of Inversion of Control with MEF and Unity.

MEFedMVVM is an open-source project hosted on *http://www.codeplex.com*, and download-able from *http://mefedmvvm.codeplex.com/*. It currently has full support for both WPF and Silverlight 4.

The feature that distinguishes this framework from other MVVM frameworks is the Attribute pattern applied to every class. This Attribute pattern transforms these classes into a pluggable ViewModel or component for MVVM. For example, to create a ViewModel class in MEFedMVVM, you just need to implement the following code:

```
[ExportViewModel("MyViewModel")]
public class MEFViewModel
{
    // implementation of the ViewModel
}
```

At this point, the *ViewModelLocator* attached to the view will resolve this ViewModel. You will be able to declare the ViewModel in your XAML View just by using the attached properties provided by this toolkit, as follows:

```
<UserControl
    <-- XAML namespaces -->
    MEFed: ViewModelLocator.ViewModel = "MyViewModel">
```

Using this approach, MEFedMVVM provides a partial mechanism for dependency injection so that your ViewModels can declare dependent services and components, and you do not need to worry about their creation. For example, the following code uses MEF to inject services into a specific ViewModel class:

```
[ExportViewModel("MyViewModel")]
public class MEFViewModel
{
    [InportingConstructor]
    public MEFViewModel(IMyService myService){
        // store the myService instance ...
    }
}
```

MEFedMVVM provides a set of facilities right out of the box for implementing the MVVM pattern. Of course, it is a lighter framework than the MVVM Light Toolkit, and it has a different approach that's oriented more toward the Inversion of Control (IoC) pattern. MEFedMVVM includes the following components:

- Attribute pattern to decorate a ViewModel class

- Full integration with MEF

- Design-time support for Visual Studio

Cinch, by Sacha Barber

Cinch is another MVVM open-source framework, created by Sacha Barber, who is an MVP for Visual C#. He writes numerous articles about both C# and WPF. Cinch is available on CodePlex at *http://cinch.codeplex.com/*, and is compatible with both WPF and Silverlight.

Cinch has a number of features, including:

- Flexible creation of editable ViewModel objects that include validation support and UI error notification

- Complete set of *WeakEvent* managers as well as an implementation of the Mediator pattern

- Threading helpers that simplify interaction between the UI and calls on other threads

- Support for various IoC frameworks and for MEF

Cinch deserves your time and attention. One way to keep up with the framework's progress is to read Sacha Barber's articles, which discuss features and the various versions of the tool. Uunfortunately, Cinch isn't yet integrated with Visual Studio 2010, and it takes a significant amount of time to fully understand its mechanisms and structure.

You can find a full set of tutorials written by Sacha at *http://www.codeproject.com/KB/WPF/ Cinch.aspx*.

MVVM and XAML Facilities

The MVVM pattern is not terribly complicated; what is complicated is the knowledge required by the technology you plan to use. For example, if you're planning to create an MVVM application using WPF, you need to have some deep knowledge about how WPF works—and that's time-consuming. Whenever you work with a specific UI technology such as WPF or Silverlight, you must learn that technology thoroughly to be able to use all of its power.

Another problem you might face when you will start to work with WPF or Silverlight is the process of building the UI—how does it work and how do you optimize it? In XAML, you can lay out a set of UI controls on a View in many different ways. For example, you can lay out controls using a *StackPanel*, a *GridPanel*, and so on.

Through the .NET community, I have found some very useful open-source tools that I personally use in my daily work, and that can make your life much easier. There are tools to provide additional IntelliSense to Visual Studio; tools to prepare a set of base classes required by the MVVM pattern; and tools to provide wizards and facilities that your MVVM application will require.

This section does not include all the available tools provided by the .NET communities and by the open-source projects; it mentions only some of them, the ones that I know and that I have seen in action. So I urge you to explore the open-source communities yourself, to find new—and perhaps even better—tools than the ones mentioned here.

Karl Shifflett's Tools

I met Karl not long ago at Microsoft, in Seattle, at a Microsoft patterns & practices annual meeting. I found his contribution on the WPF community to be essential; he's employed at Microsoft as a program manager for the patterns & practice Prism project, about which I'll discuss more on page 186. Karl has produced three major projects so far that can make the life of a WPF/SL programmer much easier. These three projects are:

XAML Power Toys

XAML Power Toys is a set of enhancements for Microsoft Visual Studio 2008 and Visual Studio 2010 that enrich the WPF/SL designers and XAML editor. It provides:

- A set of wizards to visually create and layout an XAML view

- A set of base classes and wizards to create ViewModels and Command objects

- Similar features for Silverlight

You can download XAML Power Toys from *http://karlshifflett.wordpress.com/ xaml-power-toys/*.

XAML Editor

The XAML Editor is a powerful and useful XAML IntelliSense add-in that enriches the native XAML IntelliSense that is packaged with Visual Studio by adding filters and other functionality. When you write XAML code using this add-in, the contextual IntelliSense is more obvious, and the user interface has some additional and very useful features.

You can download XAML Editor by using the Visual Studio Extensions manager, or from *http://visualstudiogallery.msdn.microsoft.com/1a67eee3-fdd1-4745-b290-09d649d07ee0/*.

In the Box Tutorial (MVVM)

In the Box is a set of tutorials embedded inside the Visual Studio UI that provide training on specific topics, such as MVVM, by reading a document and interacting with the corresponding code in the same Visual Studio instance that runs the tutorial. Karl Shifflett recently published the first tutorial that uses this approach. It is available from *http://karlshifflett. wordpress.com/2010/11/07/in-the-box-ndash-mvvm-training/*. The download provides a full set of tutorials and guidelines in C# that cover writing a WPF MVVM application from beginning to end.

Radical, by Mauro Servienti

Mauro Servienti is an Italian Microsoft MVP for Visual C# and a friend of mine. He is a frequent speaker at events for the .NET Italian community and an evangelist for the MVVM pattern.

On his blog (*http://www.topics.it/*), you will find a wealth of useful information about MVVM. Even more absorbing is how he approaches some of the features lacking in MVVM by architecting clever and useful solutions.

In 2010, Maruso decided to publish a "set of facilities" (which is not just a set of facilities in my opinion) on CodePlex. He named this toolset "Radical." You can download Radical from *http://radical.codeplex.com.*

You might wonder why I am drawing your attention to a specific set of C# facilities when you can find hundreds of them on CodePlex with the same purpose. The answer is that Radical takes a different approach; that's why I like to use it during my daily activities. Radical provides a unique set of tools specifically aimed at aiding the correct implementation of the MVVM pattern. For example, one set of tools called Memento lets you create objects with Undo/Redo capabilities. The following listing shows a simple implementation of this service:

```
IChangeTrackingServiceProvider provider = ChangeTrackingServiceProvider.GetCurrent();

provider.CreateTrackingService();
IList<Person> list = new EntityCollection<Person>();
Person p = new Person();
p.FirstName = "Mauro";
p.LastName = "Servienti";
list.Add( p );

IChangeTrackingService svc = provider.GetTrackingService();
if( svc.IsChanged ) {
    svc.RejectChanges();
}
```

Another interesting tool is an *IMonitor* with the *DelegateCommand*, a combination of a concrete implementation of the *ICommand* interface (for WPF and Silverlight) and an Observer pattern that uses *WeakEvents* to update the Command execution verification.

```
var command = DelegateCommand.Create()
    .OnCanExecute( o => true )
    .OnExecute( o => { } )
    .TriggerUsing( PropertyChangedObserver
                    .Monitor( this )
                    .HandleChangesOf( vm => vm.IsValid ) );
```

The toolset is well designed, and it provides numerous features. Exploring Radical is well worth your time, and Mauro is always willing to provide support. Here's a brief list of features available with Radical:

- Extension methods and helpers for a wide variety of situations, including LINQ, lists, objects, and more

- Implementation of a Message broker (Publisher/Subscriber) engine

- Base classes for domain entities

- Observers that can monitor object states

- A threading manager that uses a convenient fluent interface approach

- Validators and code contracts that use a fluent interface

- A plethora of XAML extensions, helpers, behaviors, UI effects, converters, and more

Composite UI Frameworks

As you have seen in this book, when you build a WPF/Silverlight application, implementing the MVVM pattern is only one part of the process; you also need to implement a persistence mechanism—a way to keep the Business Logic Layer loosely coupled to the rest of the application, and a mechanism for orchestrating the UI.

The MVVM pattern defines a methodology to separate the UI from the presentation for applications built using WPF/Silverlight or Windows Phone 7 but it doesn't explain how to orchestrate the UI, how to compose it, how to open communications between two or more views, and other tasks related to the UI.

The term "Composite UI Framework," introduced and applied by the Microsoft patterns & practices team with the Composite Application Block (CAB) project, covers a set of facilities, frameworks, patterns, and guidelines that will help you build applications using loosely-coupled components that can evolve independently from the rest of the application. CAB is developed and optimized for the Windows Form technology, while Prism is developed for WPF and Silverlight.

The Prism projects represent a considerable investment in effort on the part of Microsoft toward a Composite UI Framework. One valid alternative to Prism is Caliburn, a simpler—but less powerful—framework for building composite UI applications using WPF or Silverlight.

Microsoft Prism

Prism is a comprehensive and well-architected framework for building a composite UI. The latest version (version 4) works with WPF, Silverlight and Windows Phone 7. It provides a set of guidelines and a complete framework with which you can build modular and loosely-coupled applications, saving a lot of time and effort. The entire infrastructure is available as two .dlls provided with the project. An additional resource is the active CodePlex community, which shares documentation, tutorials, and provides discussion forums.

CodePlex also hosts the source code and binaries for Prism, at *http://compositewpf.codeplex.com/*. This section provides only a brief overview of how this complex framework works, so you'll want to download PRISM and explore it further yourself to gain a full understanding of its capabilities.

Here's the summary Prism framework description from MSDN (*http://compositewpf.codeplex.com/*):

> *Prism provides guidance designed to help you more easily design and build rich, flexible, and easy to maintain Windows Presentation Foundation (WPF) desktop applications and Silverlight Rich Internet Applications (RIAs) and Windows Phone 7 applications. Using design patterns that embody important architectural design principles, such as separation of concerns and loose coupling, Prism helps you to design and build applications using loosely coupled components that can evolve independently but which can be easily and seamlessly integrated into the overall application. Such applications are often referred to as composite applications.*

Figure 7-2, from the MSDN website, shows the structure of a Composite application built using Prism.

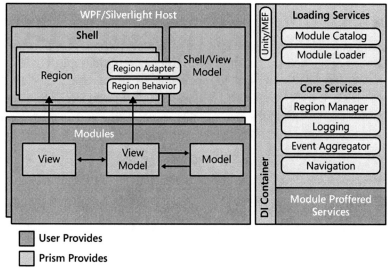

FIGURE 7-2 Architectural design of a Prism application.

Figure 7-2 shows that a Prism application is usually composed of a set of components that typically characterize the structure of a composite or modular application. These components are:

- **Shell and Regions**   The shell is the host application into which modules are loaded, while the regions are the logical placeholders used to define locations where a View will be loaded in the UI.

- **Modules and Module Catalog**   Modules are packages of functionality that can be developed and tested independently. The catalog is responsible for orchestrating the loading process of these modules.

- **Event aggregator**   This is the concrete implementation of the Publisher/Subscriber pattern that allows communication between the Views.

- **IoC and Services**   In Prism, the Services are components used to encapsulate non-UI functionality, and the IoC is used to inject these services in the application components.

Prism is not only a composite UI application framework, as already discussed, but it also provides, out of the box, guidelines and tutorials for implementing the MVVM pattern. Many developers trying to get started with Prism are discouraged by the huge amount of documentation and samples provided with this application framework, leading them to believe that Prism is too complex and not easy to use. However, that's not true. Prism is both easy to learn and easy to implement. After you start working with it, however, you will not want to return to a more traditional multiview or MDI application, because you will find that you miss all the facilities and functionality that Prism provides.

Calcium SDK

Calcium is an open-source WPF and Silverlight (alpha release) composite application toolset that takes advantage of the Composite Application Library. It provides much of what you need to build multifaceted and sophisticated modular applications rapidly. Calcium consists of a client application and server-based WCF services, which support interaction and communication between clients. Out of the box, Calcium comes with a host of modules and services, and a ready-to-use infrastructure.

Calcium is hosted on a dedicated website, *http://calciumsdk.net/*, and it's a free download. The Calcium website includes links to useful videos and getting-started tutorials.

The CalciumSDK includes the following features that enhance the Prism framework:

- Advanced module management and Module Manager for enabling or disabling modules at runtime.

- Visual Studio templates for rapidly creating Calcium projects, including client applications, MVVM Module Templates, and server WCF host projects (for both C# and VB.NET).

- Theme Support, with two attractive themes included.

- Duplex messaging services that use the same API for interacting with users from either the client or server. For example, you can interact with the user from the server by causing message boxes to appear on the client!

- Advanced commanding support, with content interfaces that determine enabled commands and views.

- Region Adapters for Toolbars and Menus.

- Client-server logging that works out of the box.

- Prebuilt modules, including a web browser, text editor, output window, and many more.

- Tabbed interface with dirty file indication (reusable across modules).

- A User Affinity module that assists in creating collaboration features so users of the application can interact.

- Undo/Redo/Repeat task management system.

Caliburn

The last framework discussed in this book is Caliburn, an open-source project hosted on CodePlex at *http://caliburn.codeplex.com/*. Caliburn was introduced to WPF developers at around the same time Microsoft released the first version of Prism.

At the beginning, due to missing features in Prism, Caliburn gained a large audience, because it was the first framework for building composite UI application with WPF. Lately, Caliburn has been losing adherents; in my opinion, that's because Prism now provides more features.

For those who don't need the full complement of features, Caliburn also ships in a micro version called Caliburn.Micro, available at *http://caliburnmicro.codeplex.com/*.

Caliburn doesn't either require or even suggest that you use a specific presentation pattern with WPF or Silverlight; it works with and provides examples for MVC, MVP, and MVVM. Caliburn's main purpose is to simplify the creation of composite UI applications, and to make it easier to test your UI and presentation layer.

In Caliburn, the application is driven by the Presenter, which in MVVM is the ViewModel component. The ViewModel is associated with a corresponding XAML View, and the bootstrapper or IoC container are in charge of resolving and associating these objects.

The latest version of Caliburn works with MEF and introduces the concept of "Decoration Attributes" to resolve dependencies such as you've already seen in the section on the MEFedMVVM toolkit.

All in all, Caliburn is a composite UI framework that's very close to Prism, but it's an open-source project that's evolving somewhat more slowly than Prism.

Index

Symbols

.NET
  categories 77
  CLR 4
  distributed data
    layers 108
  event programming 168
  generics 105
  IDataErrorInfo
    interface 164
  INotifyPropertyChanged
    interface 162
  InRule 136
  LINQ query language 96
  LOB applications xi
  O/RMs 100, 122
  Rule Engine and Business
    Rule Engine 136
  WF 4 125
_ (underline) character
  Menubar 11

A

abstract factory method 72
abstract factory pattern 27
Action<T> 174
Active Record 67, 136
adapter pattern 27
Add method 116
AddOrder method 128
AddProduct method 89
Address entity 84
ADO.NET 95
ADO.NET Entity Data
  Model 95
ADO.NET Entity Object
  Generator 95
ADO.NET Self-Tracking
  Entity 96

aggregate roots,
  defined 63
agnostic Views 29
alerts 13
Alexander, Christopher, design patterns 26
annotations, data
  annotations 77
AppFabric 132
Approval process 89
architectural design
  patterns
  classification 26
aspect-oriented program-
  ming languages 18
ASP.NET MVC, MVC
  pattern 32, 34
attributes
  attribute pattern in
    MVVM classes 182
  Data Modeling
    Attributes 77
  Display Attributes 77
  domain entities
    validation 77
  InjectionConstructor
    attribute 48
  Validation Attributes 77
Auto-Mapper 66
automatic mapping 120

B

BaseLogger class 45
behavior and state 70
behavior patterns 28
Behaviors SDK 6
binding
  dummy ViewModel to the
    View 154

ViewModel properties to
  the View Controls to
  a UI Designer 152
ViewModel to the
  View 151
View to the command
  proffered by the
  ViewModel 157
blendability, a dummy
  ViewModel 152
BLL (Business Logic
  Layer) 127
  AppFabric 132
  Business Transactions 143
  use of 137
BLL habits 138
bootstrap 174
bootstrapper method 171
bridge pattern 27
browsers, MVC pattern 33
Bugnion, Laurent 180
Build command 139
builder pattern 27
bulk operations, O/RM 94
Business Context, domain
  model 89
Business Layer 123–148
  about 123
  BLL habits 138
  Business Rules by
    Service 127
  Business Rules by
    workflow and WF
    4.0 129–133
  Business Rules versus Vali-
    dation Rules
    124–127
  Model 155
  Sample Code: the
    Business Service
    Layer 139–147

About the Author

Raffaele Garofolo is a .NET software architect who builds Line of Business applications for a living. He is passionate about .NET and Windows Presentation Foundation and spends his free time writing articles and blog posts about Windows Presentation Foundation and the MVVM (*http://blog.raffaeu.com*).

What do you think of this book?

We want to hear from you!

To participate in a brief online survey, please visit:

microsoft.com/learning/booksurvey

Tell us how well this book meets your needs—what works effectively, and what we can do better. Your feedback will help us continually improve our books and learning resources for you.

Thank you in advance for your input!

Stay in touch!

To subscribe to the *Microsoft Press® Book Connection Newsletter*—for news on upcoming books, events, and special offers—please visit:

microsoft.com/learning/books/newsletter

CPSIA information can be obtained at www.ICGtesting.com
Printed in the USA
BVOW081437250412

288663BV00007B/34/P

9 780735 650923